SOMETHING OVERHEARD

BRF encourages regular informed Bible-reading as a means of renewal in the churches.

BRF publishes daily readings with explanatory notes:
Series A for adult readers with some knowledge of Scripture;
Series B brief notes for adults, with Bible passages printed;
Compass readings and work-book, for junior children;
Discovery for young adults and beginners, with Bible passages printed.

BRF also publishes introductory booklets on Bible-reading, group study guides, children's aids, audio-visual material, etc.

SOMETHING OVERHEARD

*An Introduction
to the New Testament*

A. E. HARVEY

THE BIBLE READING FELLOWSHIP

ST MICHAEL'S HOUSE
2 ELIZABETH STREET
LONDON SW1W 9RQ

First published 1977

© BRF 1977

ISBN 0 900164 41 7

Front cover design: Haro Hodson

Printed in Great Britain by Billing & Sons Limited,
Guildford, London and Worcester

Contents

Preface

This short Introduction to the New Testament is written in the conviction that it is possible to present the methods and achievements of modern New Testament scholarship to any interested layman in such a way that he will feel able to join in the same study and to pursue the same quest. No knowledge is presupposed, no technical terms are used. The reader needs only to have a copy of the Bible to hand. The lists of passages suggested for study at the end of each chapter are by no means complete or exhaustive, and are intended only to encourage the reader to form his own opinion and to carry his own enquiry further.

The form and content of the book were shaped when I had the opportunity of giving a course of introductory lectures to a group of lay people who were training to be Lay Readers in the Diocese of Canterbury. I owe a great deal to their patience, to their sustained interest, and (not least) to their criticisms and objections.

A. E. HARVEY

Wolfson College, Oxford
September 1977

The world of the New Testament

1 Overhearing a Conversation

A few years ago a sensational discovery was made by archaeologists just outside Jerusalem. In an ancient Jewish burial ground they found the bones of a young man who must have died early in the first century AD. From the shape of the bones and the skull it could be inferred that he was a man of considerable intelligence and of slight, almost effeminate, physique, and was aged between thirty and forty when he died. *This man had been crucified*. The nail fixing his legs to the cross was still in position in the ankle-bones, with fragments of wood attached to it. From its exact position relative to the legs it could be inferred that his legs had been bending out either side of the cross. The bones of the legs had been broken by a blow across them. At some stage the corpse had been anointed for burial.

There is of course nothing in this discovery to suggest that these are the bones of Jesus of Nazareth, whom Christians believe to have risen bodily from the dead. These are the bones of an unknown young man who, like scores of others (as ancient historians tell us), was crucified by the Romans during their occupation of Palestine. From this point of view there is nothing remarkable about the discovery. What are significant are the details – the nails, the broken legs, the anointing. Here is another young Jew who was executed around the time of the crucifixion of Jesus and be exactly the same procedures as are described in the gospels.

'Jesus was crucified under Pontius Pilate'. There is no single fact that we know about the ancient world that is better attested than this. Christians have proclaimed it from the very earliest times without fear of contradiction, and non-Christian sources abundantly confirm it. But we can now go further. On the basis of this new archaeological evidence we can say that the detailed descriptions of this fact which we have in the four gospels are sober and accurate accounts of what must have taken place.

To this extent at least, then, the New Testament offers us not legend or pious meditation but history. Indeed, parts of it

were evidently written *as* history. Consider the third gospel and
Acts – two works of the New Testament writer whom we know
by the name of Luke. His first volume – the gospel – opens with
a formal dedication to his patron, a certain Theophilus. This
was precisely the kind of thing you would have expected to
find on the title page of any book offered for sale in a bookshop
in Rome or Athens or Ephesus; and his second volume (the Book
of Acts), again following the usual convention, duly refers
back in its opening words to the original dedication. Here, then,
is one writing at least in the New Testament which allows us
to know what sort of book we are dealing with. The writer is
offering a history of certain events to the reading public of the
Greco-Roman world.

Yet on closer inspection, even Luke's gospel (to say nothing
of other parts of the New Testament) turns out to be something
very different from what one would normally think of as
history. The crucifixion may indeed be a fact that can be
described and verified in historical terms, but for Christians it
can be mentioned only in association with another fact which
is of a different order altogether: the resurrection. That Jesus
rose from the dead is a matter not of historical certainty but of
faith – even though the consequences of that faith in the hearts
of Christians immediately provided the data for further history-
writing. Consequently, the records of these facts cannot be intended primarily to give the reader information or to tell him a
story; they are intended to elicit faith. The point is made explicit
only at the end of the fourth gospel, but it applies equally to the
other three: 'These things are written that you may believe
that Jesus is the Christ, the Son of God' (John 20:31). That is to
say: the gospels offer, not (or not only) history, but an invitation
to accept a certain interpretation of historical facts. They tell
their story in the manner, not of a historian, but of a preacher.

Now it happens that this is something absolutely new in the
history of literature. So far as we know, no book quite like the
gospels had ever been written before. From which we can
safely deduce that the first gospel (whichever it was) was not
written as 'literature' at all. Professional writers do not make their
name with books that fit into no category, nor will booksellers
welcome volumes which belong to no particular shelf. The

gospels can have been written only because books of this new and unprecedented kind were needed in the infant Christian communities; and to understand them we shall need to understand, as best we can, what the needs of those early Christians were.

The Gospels and Acts conventionally come first in the New Testament. But the earliest writings of all are those which come next, the Letters of Paul. At first sight, these fit more easily into place. The writing of letters is as old as the art of writing itself; and the sands of Egypt have preserved papyrus sheets containing numerous letters of this period, written in Greek, and with conventional formulas at the beginning and end very similar to those in the letters of Paul. Yet again these Christian 'letters' are something new. Very few of them are addressed to individuals: in the main they were intended to be read aloud to Christian assemblies. The conventional greetings at the beginning and end are greatly expanded in order to express something of the new unity and fellowship which bound these Christians together. And although for the most part the subjects of the correspondence are specific issues and questions arising in the life of the churches concerned, these are discussed by Paul in such a way that fundamental Christian principles are explored in the process. Never before had the form of a 'letter' been used in quite this way – though virtually all the other New Testament letters follow the pattern set by Paul. To understand them, we have once again to enter imaginatively into the life of these small local congregations of men and women newly fired by the faith and empowered by the Holy Spirit. It was a church very unlike the one which most of us know today – though there are signs in most continents of a new recovery of something of that original freshness, freedom and zeal. But until we can get something of the feel of those early congregations – their hopes and fears, conflicts and discoveries – we cannot fully understand the writings of the New Testament.

There is one further factor which makes the New Testament unlike any other book which a modern reader is likely to come across. Almost all its writings take for granted a knowledge of the Old Testament. There is a number of reasons for this, but one in particular is relevant here. Commentary on the Old Testament is precisely what the first readers of the New Testament expected to find. In one respect at least Jerusalem was totally unlike any other major city of the Roman Empire: it had no libraries, no bookshops. The only books there were would always be found in the cupboard of the local synagogue. For the Jews, there was only one book, the Old Testament. The writing of any other was positively discouraged. The only kind of 'literary' activity which was respectable was some form of commentary on the Old Testament. Now of course it would be absurd to suggest that this is what the New Testament writings primarily are: they present, not just inferences from Scripture about the God of Israel, but new facts about Jesus Christ. Yet on almost every page some new interpretation is offered of some passage in the Old Testament. This will at least have had the effect of making the reader feel at home. The very newness and originality of the New Testament forms of writing will have seemed less disconcerting and less suspect by the very fact that they contained so much scriptural interpretation.

What sort of people, then, were these first-century Christians who read and listened to works of such originality, and who felt their needs and problems to have been met by the apostolic writers? We can start with a simple fact which follows from what has just been said. They were people who knew the Old Testament. This means that they were either Jews who had heard it read in the synagogue since they were children; or else they were Gentiles who had been attracted to the Jewish religion and regularly came to the synagogue to hear the reading and exposition of the Law of Moses and to learn more of this great religion. In Acts, these people are called 'God-fearers', and it was from their ranks that many of the first Christian converts were drawn. All these people will have spoken Greek, which was the common language of the eastern Roman empire, and the language in which all the New Testament writers (with varying degrees of proficiency) composed their works. It was people such as these who, as their Christian life and experience developed, called forth and made use of those extraordinarily original writings which make up the New Testament.

This does not mean, of course, that these people can take all the credit for the existence of what has now become part of

Holy Scripture. Christians believe that greater forces were at work: the writers were inspired by the Holy Spirit, and it was by divine providence that their writings came to be composed and preserved for the guidance of the church down the centuries. But it does follow from what we have said that we cannot often expect the New Testament writers to be addressing us directly. On the contrary, reading the New Testament is rather like overhearing a conversation. The technical terms it uses are seldom defined, the precise situations involved are never explained. The writers and their readers are conversing about matters they both understand, but which they have not made clear to us. They do not tell us their agenda, their problems or their presuppositions. It is only from hints and asides that we can tell what was going on, and why they said things as they did. We have to pick up these hints in order to catch the full import of what they are saying. So let us begin our study by looking at those areas where hints of this kind are most plentiful – the worship, the preaching and the teaching of those who first responded to the transforming power and sheer newness of the gospel of Christ.

2 Christians at Prayer

Let us imagine that a historian of the future is engaged on a study of the forms of worship used by Christians in the nineteen seventies, but that he is unable to lay his hands on any prayer book or form of service which was in use at that time. He then comes across an article in a magazine written by a church leader of the period, lamenting that so many churches seem to have gone to one extreme or the other with regard to 'The Peace'. Some congregations were going in for an indecorous and exaggerated kind of bear-hug, others were maintaining a stony indifference and even taking care to sit as far apart from each other as possible. From which our historian may reasonably infer that the form of service then in use contained a section called 'The Peace', during which the worshippers were expected to exchange some kind of greeting with one another.

Our own situation with regard to the earliest Christians is very similar. We can assume that from the very beginning they must have prayed and worshipped together. But no Christian prayer book was compiled until nearly two centuries later. We have no direct information about their forms of service and their public prayers. The most the New Testament offers us is an occasional hint or allusion: the few actual descriptions of worship which we find in Paul's letters or Acts tell us little about what was normally said and done. It is as if we can occasionally overhear these Christians at their worship but – most tantalizingly – we cannot quite hear what they are saying. Yet there are few things we should like to know more. For religious people are very conservative in their prayers. They do not like to keep changing the words they use in addressing God. Consequently if we could discover how Christians prayed and worshipped by the time the New Testament came to be written we could be pretty sure that this was more or less the way they had prayed and worshipped right from the beginning. We would be in touch with the very first stirrings of Christian faith and devotion.

However, our knowledge is not quite so small as might appear at first sight. The followers of Jesus were Jews, and as Jews they had learnt the traditional Jewish forms of prayer and worship. As Christians, they will of course have made some significant changes to the prayers and praises of their fathers; but they can hardly have started completely afresh. We may safely assume that the pattern of their devotion – the basic vocabulary, so to speak, of their spiritual life – remained much the same as it had always been. And it happens that we know more or less how a pious Jew prayed in the time of Jesus.

We know, for example, that one of the most frequent and characteristic of all Jewish prayers was the prayer of Blessing or Thanksgiving.

> Blessed art thou, O Lord our God, who hast brought forth bread from the earth . . . .

Literally hundreds of such Blessings and Thanksgivings have come down to us in Jewish literature, many of them of great antiquity. Now look at the opening paragraphs of some of Paul's letters. 'I thank God at all times for you . . .' (1 Corinthians); 'Blessed is the God and Father of our Lord Jesus Christ, who . . .' (Ephesians); 'We thank God the Father of our Lord Jesus Christ whenever we pray for you . . .' (Colossians). Can we doubt that the writer was thanking God in the style he had learnt since he was a boy, simply adapting the content of his thanksgiving to his new Christian experience? (And for confirmation of this, read through the first chapter of Ephesians or Colossians in the Authorized or Revised Versions, which reflect the structure of the Greek original more accurately than do more modern versions: the way the sentences are strung one after the other with no real pause is not the way a good writer writes, but it is exactly how a good leader of prayer prays!)

Or again: when the Jews were at worship they loved to sing a hymn or psalm which recited the gracious acts of God towards his people (there are a number of psalms like this, such as Ps. 105 or 136). The Christians had a tremendous new theme for such hymn-writing: the amazing act of God in sending his Son into the world. Of course they did not leave us copies of their first hymns, any more than of their first prayer books. But every now and again a New Testament writer drops a hint that he is quoting from one of them – by falling into a more poetical style, or by stringing several clauses about Jesus on to the tell-tale pronoun 'who . . .'. Passages such as Philippians 2:6-11, Colossians 1:13 ff. and 1 Timothy 3:16 are now usually thought by scholars to be fragments of such hymns. If so, they take us right to the heart of what the first Christians said and sang in praise of their new Lord.

At the same time, the Christian faith was something quite new in religion, and we would expect to find not just a modified form of traditional Jewish prayer and praise but an altogether new style of address to God. Here we come across a clue of a rather different kind. The language in which Jesus and his first followers normally spoke (and presumably prayed) was Aramaic – a Semitic language, related to Hebrew, which was a kind of *patois* very widely used in the ancient Middle East. Within a generation, by far the greatest number of those who followed Christ were people who spoke Greek, which is the language in which the whole of the New Testament is written. It was as if a sect were to start among Welsh-speaking people in Wales but were to become of such interest throughout Britain that all its standard books come to be written in English. Yet one would expect an odd word or phrase of the original language to be preserved here and there – which is just what we do find, very occasionally, in the New Testament. The significant thing is that two of these Aramaic words – and there are very few others – are words used in prayer: *Abba*, meaning 'Father'; and *Marana-tha*, meaning 'Come O Lord'. The only possible explanation is that they were words the first Christians learned to use when praying and that they were too precious and distinctive to be translated at once into another language.

'The Spirit you have received is . . . a Spirit that makes us sons, enabling us to cry "*Abba!* Father!"' (Romans 8:15). The notion that God may be addressed as 'Father' is now so familiar to Christians that it is difficult for us to realize how radical it must have seemed to the first Christians. But recent research has proved that Jewish prayers, though they often enough addressed God in a formal way as 'Father' of his people, never approached the familiarity of calling him 'Abba', which was the personal and intimate name a son used to his own father. Mark's

gospel records (14:36) that Jesus himself used this word Abba
when praying to his heavenly father; and his disciples were
evidently taught by him to do the same (hence the beginning
of the Lord's Prayer – see especially the version in Luke's gospel,
11:2). It is no accident that this fragment of Jesus' own language
is preserved in the New Testament. It reflects a spiritual experience which came to the very first Christians and has been at
the heart of Christianity ever since – the experience that, because
of Jesus Christ, we are sons of God in a new way, and can address
God with perfect confidence and intimacy as 'Father', '*Abba*'.

'*Maranatha* – Come O Lord' (1 Corinthians 16:22). A number
of Paul's letters end in a style which suggests that they were
read aloud when the congregation was gathered for worship;
and here, sure enough, is another word in Aramaic which must
have been preserved because it was one of the first prayers the
Christians used. But again, what a lot it tells us!

Discussion has raged over the question whether Jesus taught
his followers to look forward to his return, or whether this was
not rather a subsequent misunderstanding of what he said, and
that in reality Jesus brought into the world in his own person
all that mankind can ever hope to know of God. But here is
evidence that, right from the beginning, Christians prayed for
his return. Admittedly there is a sense in which this was not
new. Jews in the time of Jesus were accustomed to pray:

> May he let his kingdom rule in your lifetime . . . speedily
> and soon.

In other words, they believed it was right to pray, not just
for piece-meal improvements in the human lot here and there,
but for a new state of affairs altogether. From the Christians'
prayer we can see that they took this one step further. The new
state of affairs would be brought about by the 'coming' (in
whatever sense) of Jesus Christ. Once again, it can be no accident
that this Aramaic phrase was preserved. It shows that right from
the beginning Christians prayed, as they have prayed ever since,
for the coming of Christ.

We said at the outset that reading the New Testament is
often like overhearing a conversation. We must now add that
the conversation we overhear is sometimes a conversation with

God – that is to say, there are passages where we can say that the writers *wrote as they prayed*. But if you know how a man prays, you know a very great deal about him and about his beliefs. Here is one way in which we can know a great deal about the very first Christians, and, through them, about Jesus Christ himself.

PASSAGES FOR REFERENCE AND FURTHER STUDY

Descriptions of worship   1 Corinthians 11:23-29; 14:23-26;
   Acts 2:44-47; 4:24-31; 20:7-8
Thanksgivings   1   Corinthians   1:3 ff.; Colossians 1:3 ff.
Blessings   Romans 1:25; 9:5; Ephesians 1:3 ff.; 1 Peter 1;3 ff.
Aramaic words   *Abba*   Mark 14:36; Romans 8:15;
                    Galatians 4:6
               Maranatha   1 Corinthians 16:22; cp.
               Revelation 22:20

3 Preaching and Response

After prayer and worship, what will have been the most characteristic activity of the early Christians? We know that the
movement began with a tiny group of Jesus' followers in Jerusalem. Within a few years it had grown into a church numbering
thousands of members, spread over several countries. Clearly
the first Christians must have devoted the greater part of their
time and energy to converting others, proclaiming the faith,
spreading the gospel – in our language, preaching sermons!
Can we tell from the New Testament what these sermons were
like? For here again, if we know what a man likes to preach
about, we know a great deal about him and his beliefs. If we
can discover something about the preaching of the earliest
Christian preachers, we shall know what seemed most important
to them in the new faith, and so perhaps what should still seem
most important to us today.

The obvious place to look for such information is in Acts. The
author of the third gospel is the only one of the gospel-writers
who took the story beyond the resurrection of Jesus by adding
to his work a second volume on the history of the early church.
Very near the beginning of this second volume he seems to be
offering us an answer to precisely the question we are asking:
he reports the first two sermons that were ever preached by a
follower of Jesus (Acts 2:14-36; 3:12-26).

But before we read off from these passages in Acts the answer
to our question, we must pause to ask just what kind of reporting
this is. When Luke was recording the teaching of Jesus in his
gospel, we may assume that he was keeping as close as he could
to what people remembered of the way in which Jesus actually
taught – and we can check his record by comparing it with those
in Matthew and Mark which, though different in many details,
do show that Luke certainly was not writing out of his head.
But when we go on to Acts and come to the sermons of the
apostles, the situation is rather different. Can we assume that
people remembered these sermons as accurately as they remem-

bered the teaching of Jesus? Or that someone made a copy that
Luke was able to refer to years later? Must we not bear in mind
that historians in the ancient world were accustomed to com-
posing speeches which no one supposed to be what the main
characters actually said, but only what they were likely to have
said on any particular occasion? And in any case, are not the
passages before us in Acts far too short to have constituted real
sermons? Are they not at most summaries of what Peter may
have said?

These questions are easier to ask than to answer, and it is
beginning to look as if it may be harder to overhear the actual
preaching of the first Christians than we thought at first. But in
fact we have a kind of check on Luke's reporting from another
source. Paul, in his first letter to the Corinthians (written within
twenty years of his own conversion) writes as follows:

> And now, my brothers, I must remind you of the gospel that
> I preached to you . . . . First and foremost, I handed on to you
> the facts which had been imparted to me: that Christ died for
> our sins, in accordance with the scriptures; that he was buried;
> that he was raised to life on the third day, according to the
> scriptures; and that he appeared to Cephas, and afterwards
> to the Twelve . . . . (1 Corinthians 15:1-5).

This, of course, is not a 'sermon' at all. But (as Paul states quite
explicitly) it is a summary of all his first sermons – a preacher's
outline, we might say. And the significant thing is that, in
essentials, it agrees with the summaries of Peter's sermons in
the early chapters of Acts. The basic facts – or rather the sermon
headings – are roughly the same in each case:

— Jesus died
— was raised from the dead
— according to the scriptures
— we are witnesses.

Of course there are elaborations and modifications. We are
talking only about a skeleton scheme which each preacher must
have clothed with his own preaching style. But the same skeleton
underlies the three passages we have been looking at, and (with
certain adjustments) others besides (see especially Act 10:36–43;

Romans 1:1-4). We may say with confidence: these were the points which, above all else, the first preachers of Christianity sought to convey to their hearers.

Have we ever heard such a sermon ourselves? Well of course we have, on those occasions when the preacher has set himself the task of proclaiming the absolute fundamentals of the Christian faith. But we would all admit that by far the greater number of sermons we hear nowadays are not like this at all. Usually, when people preach about Jesus, they refer to his miracles, his parables, his character, his teaching. In other words, the material they draw on is the kind of thing we find gathered together in the gospels. But virtually none of this comes in the early summaries in Paul and Acts – indeed there is astonishingly little reference in the second half of the New Testament to any of the facts about Jesus which are recorded in the first.

All this has important consequences for us as we seek to understand the New Testament and to lay hold of the faith which caused it to be written.

First: we find that the first preachers seem not to have spent much time calling to mind the words and works of Jesus, but to have concentrated almost exclusively on the bare essentials of the faith: the crucifixion, the resurrection, the gift of the Spirit, the testimony of the first witnesses and of the Old Testament. On the rare occasions when we can overhear them preaching we always hear the same message.

Secondly: it is unlikely that any of the gospels was written (at least in its present form) until at least twenty or thirty years after the first preaching of Christianity. We might have expected that these gospels would have been a kind of amplification of the themes of those early sermons; but in fact it is only the final sections of the gospels – the narratives of the events which lead up to the crucifixion and resurrection – which correspond to them at all. It is true that it is precisely these final sections which seem (for various reasons) to contain the earliest narratives about Jesus. It may well be, in fact, that what we now call the 'Passion narrative' came into existence as a result of the telling of this story in countless early sermons. But for the rest, the gospels seem to bear little relation to 'preaching' at all, and we shall find that there were other preoccupations and concerns of the early Christians which offer a better explanation of why they came to be written.

But we must return for a moment to the preaching itself. Again, we must rid our minds of an impression which may easily be gained from much of the preaching heard today – namely, that it is a routine exercise from which no very striking results are expected. The first preachers preached quite deliberately for a *response*. According to Acts, the hearers of Peter's first sermon were moved to ask, 'Friends, what are we to do?' To which Peter replied, 'Repent and be baptized' (Acts 2:37-8). The preaching was addressed to anyone who was not yet a Christian, and the object was to convert and to bring to baptism. Does the New Testament allow us to get the feel of this decisive moment in the life of a person who was converted by the preaching?

Once again, we have no early service books to tell us exactly what was said and done. We have some descriptions of baptism in Acts, but they are too brief to give us much idea what the service was like. On just one occasion we are told that it took place by immersion in some water out of doors (Acts 8:36-9) – but we cannot assume that it was always done in this way. What we do have are, again, hints and allusions; and these do at least show how important and profound the experience was felt to be. Paul calls it 'being buried with Christ' – from which we may infer that the convert went right down into the water until it closed for a moment over his head – and finds in it a powerful symbol of the reality of a Christian's solidarity with Christ (Romans 6:3-4). Others see it as a symbol of spiritual washing, or of rebirth; and it is even possible that the whole of what we call the First Letter of Peter was originally composed as a kind of sermon or meditation inspired by an actual service of baptism. There are many questions here to which we do not have the answer: where baptism came from, what its original meaning was, how and why Jesus instituted it as a rite to be performed in the church. But from the many reverent, meditative or excited allusions to it in the New Testament we can tell that it formed as important a part of the life of the first Christian communities as it has of the life of the church ever since.

Preaching and response – two aspects of an event which was

repeated again and again in the early years of the church, and was indeed the basis of the whole Christian movement. When something so momentous is going on in the lives of men they do not usually stop to study and record it; but when, for other reasons, they are putting pen to paper, one may expect that their exhilaration and excitement will come through what they write. It is precisely this which has given to many of the New Testament writings a quality of such immediacy and power that they still arouse a response of repentance and conversion in men and women today.

PASSAGES FOR REFERENCE AND FURTHER STUDY

Preaching   1 Corinthians 15:1-7; Romans 1:1-4; Philippians 2:5-11; Acts 2:14-39; 3:12-26; 10:36-43

Baptism   Acts 8:36; Romans 6:3-4; 2 Corinthians 1:22; Ephesians 1:13; 4:30; 1 Corinthians 6:11; Galatians 3:27; Ephesians 4:24; Colossians 3:10; Titus 3:5; 1 Peter 1:22–2:3

4 How to Behave as a Christian

Prayer and worship, preaching and converting – we have seen that these were two absolutely fundamental activities of the members of the new Christian movement, and that the New Testament contains quite a lot of information about the way in which they set about them. But it demands little imagination to see that there must have been a third activity as important and as necessary to the infant Christian community as either of the other two: that of instructing new members in the faith, of discovering and enforcing the rules of conduct which were to be observed, of settling differences of opinion on important matters of faith and conduct – in short, of *teaching*. What can we overhear about this vital activity as we read the New Testament?

Once again, we have no direct answer to this question. The teaching of Jesus himself was evidently not given in such a way that it could provide either a systematic account of what Christians should believe or a clear set of rules governing how they should behave. Nor does any of the New Testament writers deliberately set himself this task. In due course a book did come to be written, called *The Teaching of the Twelve Apostles*, which was intended to meet this need; but it probably dates from at least a generation after the latest of the New Testament writings was completed. So far as the New Testament itself is concerned, we have once again to be content with hints and allusions. The most we can do is seek to listen in when we suspect that activity of this kind was going on.

Of one thing at least we can be sure. If the Christian movement was to hold together at all, there must have been, right from the start, an agreed body of teaching by which its members could be instructed in what, as Christians, they were expected to believe and how they were expected to behave. And in fact there are references to this agreed teaching. In Romans 6:17 Paul uses a phrase which in the original Greek is somewhat compressed and difficult to translate (and so probably conceals what was already a technical term) but which means something like 'the pattern of teaching which was handed down to you'. Again, in Hebrews 6:2 we read of 'teaching' concerning the basic matters of Christian faith and practice. And we know from several references that each Christian community normally contained 'teachers' (e.g. 1 Corinthians 12:28; Ephesians 4:11). But what was this 'teaching' like? Where did it come from?

We can begin to find an answer by recognizing at the outset that Christianity was not a religion that started (so to speak) from scratch. The first Christians were Jews, and as Jews they were accustomed to regard the Old Testament as an absolutely authoritative and divinely inspired rule-book governing every detail of belief and conduct. It would not have occurred to them to jettison this venerable guide just because they had become Christians. Rather was it a question of determining precisely what changes needed to be made in the rule-book in the light of the new Christian revelation. For of course some adjustments would be necessary, even some radical reinterpretations. But the Old Testament would still remain the basis of their teaching.

And this is precisely the situation which lies behind many of the ethical passages in the New Testament. The most famous example is the crisis which arose when Gentiles (who could not be expected to regard the Law of Moses as binding upon them in every detail) began to be converted to Christianity: What should be their rules of behaviour in those matters which the Jews traditionally regarded as of great importance, such as circumcision, abstention from certain kinds of food, or the observance of the Sabbath? These were precisely the issues which caused Paul to write his urgent and passionate letter to the Galatians. Later (perhaps some thirty or forty years after the crisis) the author of Acts offered a more serene account of the episode (Acts 15:1-35). Clearly a solution was not achieved without deep feelings being aroused. It is only by entering imaginatively into the minds of the men involved in this debate that we can understand those New Testament writings which were directly inspired by it. But at the same time we shall find ourselves witnessing some of the very first attempts made to work out a guide to specifically Christian doctrine and behaviour.

On this particular issue, the matter was settled in favour of

the Gentiles: converts to Christianity were not to be expected
to undertake all the religious practices which were incumbent
upon the Jews. But this solution in its turn opened up a wider
question. If gentile Christians (who were rapidly becoming the
majority in the church) were not to regard the Law of Moses as
the ultimate authority in matters of conduct, where were they
to look for guidance? By what standard was the church now to
judge how one should 'conduct oneself in the household of
God' (1 Timothy 3:15)?

It was not to be expected that there would be any quick or
easy answer to this question. If a gentile Christian was in doubt
over some moral decision, and if (as was often the case) there was
no well-remembered saying of Jesus on the subject, what was
he to do? In fact, we find that he did the only thing we could
reasonably expect him to have done: he trusted his own judgement, he followed his own conscience – a judgement and a
conscience informed, of course, by the best moral standards of
the time. For it is only in this light that we can appreciate some
of those paragraphs of moral instruction which we find in the
New Testament letters. Read, in quick succession, the following
passages:

Ephesians 5:22-6:9
Colossians 3:18-4:1
1 Peter 2:18–3:7

You will notice at once that all three follow a similar pattern:
moral exhortations are grouped under the headings of different
classes of persons addressed (husbands, wives, slaves, masters,
etc.), and a rather similar tone – sometimes with almost identical
phrases – pervades them all. In each case the author is adding
his own modifications, his own distinctively Christian intuitions;
but it is clear that underlying each passage is a conventional code
of behaviour incorporating the highest moral standards of the
time. That is to say: on moral questions these early Christian
teachers, if they had no specifically Christian teaching to offer,
simply followed the inherited wisdom of their culture.

But a modern Christian may recoil from this conclusion.
Surely, he will say, if anything is distinctive about Christianity
it is the Christian ethic! What about the Sermon on the Mount,

what about the command to love one's enemies or to turn the other cheek? Yet a moment's reflection will show that the tremendous moral challenge of this teaching can win a response only against the background of agreed standards of moral behaviour. Christian teachers needed to make sure that the members of their congregations possessed guidelines for every-day moral conduct as well as the inspiration to respond to occasional heroic challenges. And it is precisely such guidelines that we find them offering in these general 'codes' of behaviour.

But of course this is only one side of the matter. It is by no means the case that the church simply took over accepted standards of behaviour and encouraged its members to go on being decent people. More powerful and radical motives were at work. But what we see in the New Testament, once again, is not a systematic presentation of these ideas, but a series of documents – as it were minutes of meetings, letters from a correspondence, sermons preached in moments of crisis – which reveal the early Christians discovering the implications of their faith as they were confronted by different situations in their daily lives. Again and again the argument in one of Paul's letters gives us a glimpse of this process of discovery (see below, page 39). Then as now people did not always see how one's Christian faith impinges on some of the routine questions of life. But Paul helped his readers to see how their Christian faith invited them to adopt a radically Christian solution. His letters, like the New Testament as a whole, offer not a treatise on morals but a series of significant examples of the way in which Christian principles can revolutionize conduct.

Yet we still need to ask: what about the teaching of Jesus himself? Surely this must have been the basis of much of the early Christian instruction? And there are of course occasional references to it. Paul quotes, for example, Jesus' prohibition of divorce (1 Corinthians 7:10), and a saying bearing on the payment of Christian ministers (1 Corinthians 9:14). The Letter of James seems to allude to Jesus' teaching about swearing (5:12). But it remains true that explicit appeals to a ruling of Jesus are strangely few and scattered. And perhaps, when we look at the gospels, we can see why. Even the Sermon on the Mount, where the largest amount of Jesus' ethical teaching is gathered together, does not constitute any kind of treatise or rule-book for be-haviour. It shows Jesus taking issue with the standards of his contemporaries and suggesting how a more radical approach to the Law of God may affect even the most humdrum situations of daily life. 'It was said . . . but I say . . .' It is only by reflection on what is generally accepted around him that a Christian can come to see what the possibilities for Christian action may be. This was the approach to moral questions of Jesus himself and (as we can see from the New Testament letters) of his first followers. It explains why no satisfactory manual of Christian behaviour has ever been written. The challenge of Christ can be met only within the specific circumstances of an individual's life. The New Testament shows how it can be done; but it still leaves us (as the first Christians were left) with the task of working out our own moral decisions for ourselves.

PASSAGES FOR REFERENCE AND FURTHER STUDY

(a) References to 'teaching' and 'teachers'   Romans 6:17;
    1 Corinthians 12:28; Ephesians 4:11; 1 Timothy 4:6, 11;
    Hebrews 5:12; 6:2
(b) 'Codes' of behaviour   Ephesians 5:22 – 6:9;
    Colossians 3:18 – 4:1; 1 Peter 2:18 – 3:17
(c) Allusions to Jesus' teaching   1 Corinthians 7:10; 9:14;
    1 Thessalonians 4:15; Acts 20:35; James 5:12
(d) A series of moral issues   1 Corinthians 5–11

5 *According to the Scriptures*

One of the most vivid and significant finds made during the excavations at Qumran consisted of fragments of furniture from a large first-floor room. These fragments, when pieced together, revealed the existence of a table some sixteen feet long and eighteen inches wide, with a bench alongside it. Two inkwells were also found. There can be little doubt that this was indeed the room where a group of scribes worked day after day producing those famous documents which we now know as the Dead Sea Scrolls.

A great number of these documents were compositions of a particular kind. They were what we would now call commentaries on Holy Scripture. The following is a typical passage.

For behold, I rouse the Chaldeans, that bitter and hasty nation. (Habakkuk 1:6)

Interpreted, this concerns the Kittim, who are quick and valiant in war, causing many to perish.

'Kittim' appears to be a kind of code name for the Roman occupying troops, and the object of the commentaries was to show how Old Testament prophecies were being fulfilled (as the writers believed) in events of contemporary history. The writings are anonymous: we must imagine a group or 'school' of learned men engaged in the twin activities of 'searching the Scriptures' and 'discerning the signs of the times'. Their commentaries were the fruit of their conviction that they lived in a time when hidden meanings of Old Testament passages were at last being revealed in contemporary events.

Look now at Matthew's gospel. No less than nine times this evangelist introduces a quotation from the Old Testament with a formula such as

'This was to fulfil what was spoken by the prophet . . .'

And did not Jesus himself say, 'Do not think that I came to destroy the law and the prophets. I did not come to destroy but to fulfil' (Matthew 5:17)? Is it not possible that the entire gospel is an exercise in demonstrating how the coming of Jesus 'fulfilled' the prophecies of the Old Testament? Indeed, may we not go further and imagine the gospel being compiled by a 'school' of learned students – as at Qumran – who again and again found new significance in the Scriptures in the light of their new Christian experience – who were in fact Christian scribes 'bringing out of their treasure things new and old' (Matthew 13:52)?

Before we try to answer this question we must be clear precisely what is meant (in this context) by the word 'fulfil'. We tend to think of this in a very simplified way. We read in the Old Testament a statement like 'Behold a virgin shall conceive' (Isaiah 7:14). We take this as a prophetic glimpse into the future providentially granted to Isaiah; we note that it was miraculously 'fulfilled' by the birth of Jesus; and we may go on from there to argue that the truth and divinely ordered nature of the facts about Jesus are confirmed by the amazing circumstance that these facts were predicted in detail some hundreds of years earlier. Now it is true that this is how some apologists for the Christian faith have argued ever since the second century AD. It is also true that a passage such as Matthew 1:22-23 seems at first sight to be an example of just such simple reasoning. But in reality the matter is a good deal more complicated – and indeed (we may judge) more convincing.

We must note, first, that it is not nearly so easy to tell in Hebrew as it is in a European language whether a statement is a 'prediction' or not. In English, we would make the matter clear by using the future tense: 'a virgin shall conceive'. But in Hebrew the tenses are not so precise. It would be fair to translate this particular verse, 'a virgin conceives': it is left to the reader to feel instinctively from the context whether the reference is to past, present or future.

Secondly (to take this example a little further) the correspondence may not be so exact as appears at first sight. The Hebrew word translated 'virgin' in fact means simply 'girl'. The original prophecy, therefore, was a good deal less sensational than it appears in English. As translated in the NEB it runs, 'A young woman is with child'. Indeed we would not ourselves call it a 'prophecy' at all. But now we must watch how the Christian scribe (following traditional Jewish methods) seems to have gone to work on such unpromising material. He will have said to himself, in effect, that there is something suggestive about this text. 'A young woman is with child' – what young woman? Isaiah does not tell us, and there has been no woman-with-child in Jewish history to date who is significant enough to be the person alluded to in the inspired word of the prophet. Therefore (so the argument will have run), since nothing in Scripture can be false or without significance, we must conclude that the young woman has remained all this time a person of the future. But how shall we recognize this unique 'young woman' when she does appear in history? At this point a further clue is introduced. Our Christian scribe does not study the Old Testament only (if at all) in Hebrew. He also knows the translation into Greek that was made about three centuries before his time, and every word of which was regarded as being inspired like the original. In the Greek, this word 'young woman' was translated *parthenos* which usually (though not always) meant 'virgin'. Perhaps then this prophecy would be fulfilled only when that almost unimaginable thing took place – a virgin conceiving a child. But (here is the new fact which can now be brought into the picture) Mary, the mother of Jesus, was a virgin. Therefore in her, at last, the Old Testament text takes on its full meaning, that is, it is 'fulfilled'.

Such reasoning may seem to us strange and artificial. But underlying it is a very strong and profound conviction, namely, that since Holy Scripture is divinely inspired, nothing in it (however obscure at first sight) can be trivial, meaningless or irrelevant. If the significance of some text is not apparent, it may be that the event has not yet taken place which will make clear its meaning. But the Christian knew by his faith and experience that in Jesus Christ a whole new sequence of events had recently taken place of quite unique importance. Surely these would give the key to many Old Testament texts which had long remained mysterious. Or surely (to put it in the terms with which we started) many of these passages in the Scriptures were now for the first time 'fulfilled'. By studying them, the believer could be helped to fit his new Christian experience into the grand purposes of God as revealed in the Law and the Prophets.

We must therefore imagine that the Christian scribe (if it was

indeed such who compiled a composition like Matthew's gospel)
was engaged in a rather more sophisticated activity than just
matching Old Testament prophecy with Christian fulfilment.
He had first to cast about in the records of Jesus and of the
new Christian movement for facts which might be of special
significance; this was traditionally called 'discerning the signs
of the times' (Matthew 16:3). At the same time he must ponder
again all those 'open-ended' texts in the Old Testament of which
the true significance had perhaps lain hidden for centuries but
which might now be becoming plain in the light of recent
events – the traditional activity of 'searching the Scriptures'
(John 5:39). Again and again, Christian scribes found that these
things were coming together in a remarkable way. The result of
their meditation on the acts of God in their own time and of
their study of Scripture was a narrative constantly enriched by
Old Testament references, and a selection of Old Testament texts
invested with a new power to illuminate the stirring events they
were recording.

This way of seeing the matter will help us to understand what
may otherwise seem exceedingly puzzling. In one of his first
sermons, Peter is recorded as saying:

> 'What God foretold through the mouth of all the prophets,
> that his Messiah should suffer, he has now fulfilled.' (Acts 3:18)

But (we may ask) where in the prophets do we find anything
about a suffering Messiah? There is one passage, it is true, where
this may be the case. In the famous fifty-third chapter of Isaiah
there is talk of a 'suffering servant' who was perhaps later identified with the Messiah who was to come. But Peter's words are
'*all* the prophets'. Surely, if not actually false, this is at least a
gross exaggeration?

But this is again to look at the matter too simply. The Christian
interpreter was not looking in the Old Testament for precise
'predictions'. Rather he was looking for the kind of 'open-ended'
statements which might now for the first time reveal their true
meaning. Up to now, Jewish interpreters, with an idea in their
minds of a glorious and victorious national leader who would
deliver his people as the Lord's Anointed (the Messiah, the
Christ), had searched the Scriptures for the kind of text which

could be said to describe such a figure. It would never have occurred to them to draw into their study texts which described suffering and death. But the Christians, realizing that Jesus was indeed the Messiah, the Christ, by virtue of his very willingness to suffer, were able to draw on that great store of passages in prophets and psalms which describe the suffering of an innocent and godfearing man. Now at last these passages were beginning to reveal their true meaning, they had been 'fulfilled'. In this sense it was no exaggeration for Peter to say that it was foretold in all the prophets that the Messiah should suffer.

So the picture with which we began, of a 'school' of Christian scribes offering new interpretations of the Old Testament, certainly helps us to see why some parts of the New Testament are as they are. Many passages can almost be seen growing out of the excited realization that the things concerning Jesus both gave significance to, and were illuminated by, some of those 'open-ended' texts of Scripture which had never before been fully understood. Yet a moment's reflection will show that this cannot possibly be the whole story. There is much in the gospels – indeed in the New Testament as a whole – which is the product, not of meditation on familiar texts, but of an encounter with the utterly new and unique personality of Jesus. The gospels could never have been written without this decisive new factor; mere meditation on Old Testament texts would have produced something as essentially dull and lifeless as are the commentaries from Qumran. We have discerned at most one strand – though an important one – in the composition of the gospels. The Christian scribe is one who brings out of his treasure things *new* as well as old. The sheer newness of the gospels is something we must never forget, and which we shall come back to in a later chapter.

PASSAGES FOR REFERENCE AND FURTHER STUDY

'Formula quotations' ('. . . that it might be fulfilled that was spoken . . .') Matthew 1:22; 2:15, 17, 23; 4:14–16; 8:17; 12:17–21; 13:35; 27:9

New interpretations of Scripture Acts 3:22–25; 4:24–28; 8:30–35; Romans 9:24–33; 1 Corinthians 10:1–13; Hebrews 3–4; 5:5–6; 1 Peter 2:22–25

6 The Church under Attack

(a) From the Jewish side

Up to now we have been looking at some of the characteristic activities of the early Christians – their prayer and worship, their preaching and teaching, their meditation on Scripture – and noticing the traces these activities have left on the writings of the New Testament. But it is the experience of every religious movement that it is only under the pressure of attack, persecution and challenge that belief and conduct become precisely defined. It is only when our convictions are challenged that we find it necessary to say exactly what it is that we believe. Thus for a while the Christian church may well have been content to state its belief that 'Jesus is Lord, to the glory of God the Father' (Philippians 2:11 – a passage which, as we have seen, may go back to the very early years of the church's worship). But in due course it will have been challenged to say whether, in that case, it was being claimed that Jesus was equal to God (John 5:18); or whether, after all, Jesus might not be a being inferior to other supernatural powers (Colossians 2:8). Or again, if their new faith seemed to make it less important to adhere strictly to the Jewish Law, strict Jews will have attacked the Christians for being too permissive; while gentile Christians, who had never had so much respect for the Law of Moses, may well have wondered why it was necessary to continue with any of these observances at all. Such questions are usually brought to a head by some crisis. Opinions will differ for a while within the movement itself; there may be tension and bitterness. Finally the matter is settled one way or the other, and another stage is reached in the formulation of Christian belief and moral principles – a process which has continued ever since and which must continue as long as Christ is proclaimed in the world.

About a third of the New Testament consists of 'epistles' – for the most part real letters sent by church leaders to congregations, and elicited by challenges of this kind. Indeed it is only by seeking to understand what these challenges were – what matters of belief and practice were being called into question, what issues were involved – that we can understand what the writers were trying to say. Often the crisis was a local one: a particular attack was being launched against the church, a particular issue had to be settled – which is the case, as we shall see, with many passages in Paul's letters. But we can also discern certain strains and pressures to which Christians were being subjected wherever they were, and which have left a deep imprint on many different parts of the New Testament. We shall devote this and the following chapter to these.

It is natural to turn first to the Acts of the Apostles, which is the only consecutive narrative we possess of the early years of the church. We have to be a little cautious in our use of it; for if anything is clear about this early attempt at church history it is that the author, who was after all writing some years after the event, was mainly concerned to present the grand outline of the church's advance from Jerusalem to Rome; he showed less interest in those crises which (as we know from Paul's letters) were a notable feature of those early years and which for our present purpose are of particular interest. Nevertheless his narrative gives us at least a framework in which to set the various episodes we read of in more detail in other writings. The story begins with the small but rapidly growing community of Christian believers, anxious to convert their fellow-Jews to their conviction that the long-awaited Messiah had now come in the person of Jesus, and continuing in other respects to practise the Jewish faith and to be seen in the precincts of the temple in Jerusalem. The first trouble comes when Peter miraculously cures a paralysed beggar (Acts 3), and the question is at once raised by the authorities, by what power or in whose name has he done this? (4:7). For here was the point: Judaism as a religion was very tolerant of differences in theoretical belief – even the opinion that a certain person was the Messiah might be regarded as acceptable for a time. But once someone started acting unlike other people, then immediately the question would arise of his authority for doing so. Peter's answer, that his authority came from the very Jesus who had been crucified at the instigation of the Jews themselves, was hardly calculated to pacify the Jewish elders.

The next crisis touches deeper issues. Stephen, a newly appointed leader, is accused of 'speaking words against the holy place and the law' (6:13), and in his long speech of self-defence he does in effect make an attack on the whole institution of the temple (7:44-53). The interesting thing is that the kind of argument he uses is one which we know was used in some Jewish quarters, particularly among Jews of the Dispersion who believed that the whole ritual and sacrificial side of the religion should now be abandoned and that Judaism should become quite frankly identified with the moral and religious ideals taught in synagogues throughout the Greek-speaking world. It is as if, at this point, the new Christian movement was echoing the views of an already influential school of Jewish thought; but the reaction of the official Jewish authorities was vigorous, and we are told that the episode resulted not just in the death of Stephen but in a 'great persecution' (8:1) which was actually abetted by the government.

But the greatest crisis was still to come. Differences in belief and doctrine may be enough in themselves to set men at each other's throats; but far more powerful is the sense of animosity and outrage which can follow the transgression of a deep and irrational taboo. As we know so well from the racial problems of our own day, it is not so much the theoretical differences between one race or culture and another which cause trouble as the immediate practical problems which arise when members of different races live at close quarters with each other. So it was in the first Christian century. To any Jew, one of the most fundamental and deep-seated taboos which went with his religion was the absolute prohibition of sitting down for a meal with a non-Jew. Courteous and considerate as many Jews were towards their gentile neighbours, their social intercourse always stopped short of sharing a meal together – for here all those deep shibboleths came into play concerning ritual purity, the fear of uncleanness, the fear of unwittingly eating foods that, to Jews, were unlawful. It was one thing, therefore, to reach the conclusion, in principle, that non-Jews might join the Christian movement on equal terms with Jews – this point was established at an early stage (see Acts 10). But it was quite another thing to suggest that, as a result, Jews and Gentiles could begin to consort with one another socially on equal terms. Yet the central act of

Christian worship (the eucharist) was a common *meal*. How was this obstacle to be overcome?

The different stages of this crisis are clearly visible in the New Testament writings. The first stage is the theoretical one, following immediately upon the agreement in principle that Gentiles could become Christians. The question was, on what terms? How Jewish must they become? How much of the Jewish religion, how many of the Jewish taboos, must they be prepared to accept? As one would expect, opinions were divided; and Acts 15 records a formal meeting at Jerusalem at which a compromise was worked out: one or two of the traditional taboos were to be respected, but in other respects the gentile Christians were to be spared the rigorous application of the Jewish law. That was well enough in theory. We may imagine that in Jerusalem (where the decision was taken) a gentile Christian was a phenomenon that barely anyone had seen, let alone tried to integrate into a Jewish-Christian group. But meanwhile, at a city like Antioch, the situation was very different. There were at least as many Gentiles as Jews in the church, and the taboos must have been simply swept away by the enthusiasm of the majority. It was there that matters came to a head. A distinguished delegation of Christian leaders from Jerusalem visited Antioch, and when they saw Jew and Gentile sitting down at table together, they simply could not bring themselves to join in. Understandably, their traditional prejudices and their well-formed Jewish consciences were far too strong to be overwhelmed in a moment. The scene is described – not without indignation – by Paul in his letter to the Galatians (2:11-14). Characteristically, Paul saw that this was far more than a practical question of how to get the different races to sit down at table together. Any compromise would have been a deadly menace to that wonderful unity of all races and classes which is experienced in Christ, and would moreover have given their chance to the Jewish enemies of Christianity who were only too ready to exploit any racial tensions which existed within the church. The attacks of these Jewish opponents can be overheard on every page of Galatians, and explain the passion with which Paul presses home his arguments for total equality between the races within the Christian fellowship.

Paul's view prevailed, partly because of the sheer power of
his reasoning, partly because of the sensational experience of
many Jewish Christians that the new one-ness in Christ was in
fact powerful enough (as it still is today) to overcome every
racial prejudice and taboo. But one may ask, why did the question
ever arise? Did not Jesus make the point clear? Could the matter
not have been settled from the outset by simply referring to
the teaching of Jesus himself?

To which the answer is, apparently, that Jesus gave no such clear
guidance. And perhaps this is not surprising. His audience had
almost always consisted of Jews, his immediate followers were
all Jews, and the question of the co-existence of Jews and Gentiles
in a single fellowship was one that simply did not arise in his
lifetime. On the other hand, it was very soon realized that his
teaching had implications for this question. Here, in fact, is
another clue to the reason why certain episodes in the gospels
were remembered and recorded. One of the clearest instances
is the passage in which Jesus declares that it is what comes out of
a man's mouth, not what goes in, which makes him unclean.
'This he said', adds the account in Mark's gospel, 'making all
foods clean' (7:19). Here we overhear precisely the debate which
was going on when the gospel was written: did any of the
Jewish food laws apply to gentile Christians? And an answer is
found in a saying of Jesus which (though its original point was
probably somewhat different) might seem to settle the matter.
Or again, Jesus was undoubtedly involved in disputes with the
Jewish authorities about the proper observance of the sabbath.
But now, the question kept cropping up whether non-Jewish
Christians should be bound by this Jewish observance. Surely
there would be at least a hint of an answer in what Jesus said
about it? And we find, again, that some of these sabbath episodes
are clearly narrated with an eye on the argument going on at
the time.

Here then is another factor which caused the New Testament
to be written in the way that it was. The church was under
pressure: the Jewish community saw with dismay that some of
its members were joining the new movement and apparently
beginning to sit light to some of the customs which any good
Jew regarded as absolutely binding. The Jewish attack on the

church was the more insidious in that it awoke a response in the consciences of many Jewish Christians who were led to question whether after all their new-found Christian freedom was according to the will of God. It was met by some powerful theological arguments in Paul's letters to the Galatians and the Romans – indeed without it we should never have had those two magnificent epistles; and it caused Christian believers to call to mind instances in the activity and teaching of Jesus which would give them the assurance they needed that they were on the right path. We may say that this is one more strand woven into the complex texture of those records of the life and work of Jesus which were written in the second half of the first century AD in response to the needs of the church – the four gospels.

PASSAGES FOR REFERENCE AND FURTHER STUDY

Problems arising from the conversion of Gentiles
(a) circumcision   Acts 15; Galatians 1 – 2;
   cp. Colossians 2:11; Ephesians 2:11–22
(b) food laws   Acts 15; Galatians 2:12; Mark 7:14-23
(c) theological questions   Mark 12:28-34; Mark 11:17;
   Matthew 5:17-18; Galatians 6:15; Philippians 3:3;
   1 Peter 2:9-10

7 The Church under Attack

(b) From the Gentile side – Revelation and 1 Peter

The early Christians were threatened, harassed, and at times even physically assaulted by their Jewish neighbours: so much is clear from many passages in the New Testament. At least one of their leaders was actually killed – Stephen, the first Christian martyr. But none of this amounts to what we would normally call 'persecution', if by that we mean a systematic attack on the persons of Christians for the sole reason that they professed the Christian faith. Such an attack could not have been launched by the Jews alone; it would have needed the assistance of the State – that is, ultimately, of Rome. Our question must now be: did the Roman government persecute the church during the period in which the New Testament was written?

This is by no means merely an academic question of history. Persecution is not just a tribulation that members of a new sect may have to undergo. It does something to their faith, and (which is still more to the point for our present purpose) it tends to stimulate their thinking and writing. This was certainly the case in Jewish literature. The literary *genre* known as 'apocalyptic' began to be used in earnest in the second century BC, at a moment which looked like being the darkest hour in Jewish history – the moment when a pagan ruler, Antiochus Epiphanes, attempted to paganize the Jewish religion by force. Out of this crisis of persecution came the Book of Daniel. Part of this book recalls heroic legends of old intended to show how God never abandons those who hold firm to their faith and their ancestral laws; the other part is a series of visions (again attributed to the same hero of the past, Daniel) which describe in highly symbolic form the tribulations of the writer's own time and the ultimate victory of which God's people can be assured. It was this latter part which became the model for numerous subsequent 'apocalypses' – the word means simply the revelation of the future course of events as seen by some privileged visionary – and the purpose of these works was to give consolation and hope to those who were facing persecution for their faith. The New Testament contains a major example of the *genre* – the Revelation of John. Was this 'apocalypse' also inspired by the outbreak of persecution against the Christians?

Oddly enough this question is not at all easy to answer. The only official persecution of which we have independent evidence is the famous occasion in AD 64 when the Emperor Nero turned on the Christians in Rome as scapegoats for the great fire of that year. Both Peter and Paul are believed to have lost their lives in this outbreak of deliberate persecution. But it happens (if the usual dating of the New Testament writings is even roughly correct) that no book of the New Testament was written at this time; and in any case the persecution was short-lived. After that, we have nothing firm to go on until, around AD 112, the Roman writer Pliny, in the course of his official duties as a provincial governor in Asia Minor, had a correspondence with the Emperor Trajan which allows us to glimpse the considerable pressure which was being put on the Christians by the Roman government. This was indeed persecution: men and women were being executed for refusing to worship the Emperor. But it is after our period; the New Testament was probably complete by the time of Trajan. And between Nero and Trajan we have virtually nothing to go on.

Pliny does, however, make mention of one or two Christians who had recanted (presumably under pressure) twenty years previously. That brings us back to the early nineties of the first century – the reign of Domitian – and to a period which is a plausible date for the writing of the Book of Revelation. At first sight this fits very well. The author, as he says himself, is in exile (1:9); we read of one Christian who has evidently died a martyr's death (2:13); and some of the thinly veiled descriptions of the malign power of the Roman administration suggest that it was certainly something to be afraid of if you were a Christian (17:6). Yet we must be careful not to read too much into these passages. There are surprisingly few references in Revelation to Christians actually suffering persecution; the horror inspired in the writer's mind by the Roman civilization is more a revulsion from its paganism and idolatry than a hatred inspired by fear; and in the letters to the seven churches, with which the book begins, there is much more concern with the danger from within – heresy, apostasy and the inevitable cooling off of the first ardour of faith – than with any threats from without. The *form* of the Book of Revelation is certainly derived from the tradition of Jewish apocalyptic writings; but the content is not such that it would be fair to say that it must have been written under stress of actual persecution.

There is another writing in the New Testament which seems – again at first sight – to indicate that a persecution has been launched against the church. 'Do not be bewildered', writes the author of the First Letter of Peter, 'by the fiery ordeal that is upon you' (4:12). One's mind travels at once to Rome, where the story is that Nero coated Christians with tar and set light to them like torches along the road. And if St Peter was in fact a victim of that outbreak of persecution, may this not be an allusion to the terrible scenes he was witnessing? Moreover a few verses later the writer talks of 'suffering as a Christian' and 'confessing the Name' (4:15 NEB), phrases which are startlingly like those used half a century later by Pliny when he writes about the official Roman policy towards Christians.

But again, we must be careful not to jump to any quick conclusions. If this is indeed a letter written under stress of actual persecution it is surprising how *few* references the author makes to it – for in fact the greater part of the letter is about other things altogether. Moreover – though the question is far from settled – many would say that the letter is very unlikely to have been written by the apostle Peter himself, or even within ten years of his death. And finally, we must face the fact that a phrase like 'fiery ordeal' is one that had long been used in a rather literary way to describe any circumstance which put a man's faith to the test. In other words, we may say that it is *possible* that 1 Peter was written under conditions of persecution; but we can hardly go much farther than that.

It may be then that none of the New Testament writings is a 'persecution document' in quite the way that, say, the Book of Daniel is. But this does not mean that the pagan world of the Roman Empire did not exert other threats against the Christian communities scattered in its territories. Christians may not have been frequently exposed to the danger of losing their lives for their faith – the first major persecutions belong to the following century – but they were certainly subject to more subtle strains and pressures from their pagan environment, and were forced by circumstances to take up a definite attitude towards it. And this situation has certainly left its mark on their writings.

The most vivid example of this is again the Book of Revelation. We have already seen that the form of this book was inspired by a long tradition of so-called 'apocalyptic' Jewish writing, in which one may expect to find cryptic and symbolic references to events contemporary with the writer woven into the texture of a visionary and long-term view of history. Many of these references are inevitably obscure and problematical to us today. But in a more general way we can certainly read off from these pages what it felt like to be a Christian in the midst of a pagan society, and what the writer's attitude was. To a Jew, with his passionate belief in a single creator-God who could be represented by no man-made image (and this jealous monotheism was inherited by all Christians, whether or not they were Jews), one of the most shocking and repellent features of any gentile city in the Roman Empire was the presence of innumerable statues of all the different gods to whom the citizens offered sacrifices, libations and prayers. Jewish literature from the great prophets onwards (see for example Isaiah 40:18-20) produced endless variations on the theme of the sheer folly and perversity of men who worshipped gods of gold and silver and stone (sometimes, it is true, rather missing the point that a devout pagan did not of course worship the statues themselves, but the gods he believed they represented). Add to this a development which was taking place during the century in which the New Testament was written: the Roman Emperor himself was attributing divine nature and honours, first to his dead predecessor (which was bad enough), and then (which seemed outrageous to any sensitive monotheist) to himself while still alive. Statues of emperors, then, were being placed next to statues of gods, and were becoming the object of sacrifices and prayers; and a Christian, if he were unlucky enough to be challenged about his religion, might be compelled (this was the ultimate horror) on pain of death to offer such a sacrifice himself. No wonder the author of the Book of Revelation found reason to revive the old imagery of 'beasts' standing for pagan powers, one of which could 'cause all who would not worship the image to be put to death' (13:15). No wonder Rome became identified in his mind (and in that of the author of 1 Peter) with that archetype of all sacrilegious cities – Babylon! (17:1-6; 1 Peter 5:13).

But there were other aspects of paganism which caused equal concern and revulsion. The Jews (and following them the Christians) held a strict code of behaviour in sexual matters, and the much more permissive society of the Greco-Roman world seemed shocking and threatening to their own inherited attitudes. In particular, the indulgent attitude towards homosexual practices which characterized most Greek-speaking cities appeared no better than a perversion to members of the strictly heterosexual Jewish culture. The first chapter of Romans contains an absolutely typical expression (verses 25-32) of the normal Jewish attitude to the *mores* of pagan society, and is written with all the more earnestness in that it seemed vital to Jewish Christians that their newly converted Gentile brothers should not bring with them into the church any of that licentiousness which a Jew involuntarily associated with the social life of his pagan neighbours. New Testament writers, from Paul in his earliest letters to the author of the First Letter of John (written perhaps a generation later) insist again and again that, by becoming a Christian, one has entered a society where such conduct is simply unthinkable.

Yet if that were all there was to it, the young church would look depressingly like one of those religious sects which seem to disapprove so heartily of the society all round them that they become aloof, isolated and ultimately irrelevant. But in fact the Christians had positive as well as negative things to say about the Roman Empire. In particular, they appreciated its greatest gift to their own troubled part of the world – peace and order. 'We must be obedient', writes Paul in a famous chapter of Romans (ch. 13). 'Honour the Emperor', writes the author of 1 Peter (2:17). Even if there was to be no compromise with the religion and morals of the pagan world, at the same time there was to be no question of rebelling against its authorities or withdrawing from the ordinary duties of citizenship. Paying taxes, respecting magistrates, praying for pagan rulers – all these public-spirited attitudes are inculcated in those New Testament writings which are addressed (as so many of them were) to congregations which needed guidance on how to behave on all those delicate occasions when their new religion seemed to put them to some extent at risk. Christians are not *of* the world, but they are *in* the world; and many passages in the New Testament show us – indeed take their origin from – situations where the proper Christian response to the needs and demands of the world around was being worked out in the light of their new-found faith that 'God wills all men to be saved'.

PASSAGES FOR REFERENCE AND FURTHER STUDY

Persecution   1 Thessalonians 2:14; 1 Peter 4:12; Revelation 1:9; 2:13; 17:6

Moral judgements on paganism   Romans 1; Colossians 3:5–8; 1 Peter 4:3–5

Attitudes to the State   Mark 12:13–17; 13:9–10, 14; Romans 13; 1 Peter 2:13–17

8 Paul

Up to now we have been talking of 'New Testament writers' in general terms, as if they were men about whom we know little or nothing except that they are the authors of certain epistles or gospels. And broadly speaking this is true. The names attached to the four gospels – Matthew, Mark, Luke and John – tell us little or nothing about their authors (who may or may not be the same persons as bear these names in the narratives themselves), and the men who wrote the letters of Peter, James and John, and the Letter to Hebrews, are at best shadowy figures about whom we can say little more for certain than that their literary styles differ somewhat from one another. But to this there is one notable exception – the apostle Paul. In all the literature that has come down to us from antiquity there are few writers whose personality makes such a vivid impact on us as his. Here indeed is a writer of flesh and blood.

We know Paul as the author of the most personal and passionate letters in the New Testament. But we also have an independent portrait of him by another writer. Paul is the hero of the whole of the second half of the Acts of the Apostles. There we can read of his sensational conversion; we can follow the course of his arduous but amazingly successful missionary journeys; we can read his speeches and sermons (though these may owe much of their style and even of their content to the hand of the narrator); and we can study his reactions to all the various adventures which befell him – including his nearly fatal shipwreck. Perhaps at first sight it may seem something of a disappointment, when we turn to Paul's own letters, that we find so few pages in them concerned with these exciting events. Rather Paul's preoccupation as he takes up his pen is almost always with the continuing life of the churches he has founded and the maintenance of his own warm relationship with them. Yet in the long run this preoccupation has yielded more inspiration and solid gain to subsequent generations of Christians than would have been the case had he filled his letters with personal anecdotes.

Not that his interest in the affairs of his churches makes his letters any less personal. 'Therefore, my friends, beloved friends whom I long for, my joy, my crown . . .' (Phil. 4:1); 'You would have torn out your very eyes, and given them to me . . .' (Galatians 4:15); 'I wish you would bear with me in a little of my folly . . .' (2 Corinthians 11:1). This is not the style of a formal preacher or theologian, but of a man who puts all his heart as well as his mind into his writing. Paul is always personally concerned for those to whom he addresses his letters, and it is this passionate involvement which allows us so often to glimpse the nature of the man as he really was. Paul the tireless missionary, Paul the sensitive pastor, Paul the strict disciplinarian, the ascetic, the fighter, the mystic – all these aspects of his personality are known to us through the sheer candour and spontaneity of his writing.

Yet the greatness of Paul's letters is that, starting from the circumstantial and the relatively trivial, they so often rise to a level from which one gains a view of the most vital matters of the Christian faith. 1 Corinthians is perhaps the most perfect object-lesson in this. Paul has heard, both by letter and by word of mouth, of all kinds of crises and tensions which have begun to disturb the life of the church in Corinth. Most of these disputed questions could have been settled by practical wisdom and common sense – as Paul himself recognizes. But again and again the genius of Paul shows itself when he sees the deeper implications of the question and, by revealing to his readers how their Christian faith bears upon it, helps them to see both themselves and their faith in a new light. Take, for example, the fact that the Corinthians were becoming litigious and taking each other to law in pagan courts. It was easy enough for Paul to point out to them that this was not the way any religious society should behave: they should surely be able to settle their differences among themselves! (6:1-6) But then Paul takes his argument a step further. He asks them to look at what they are doing in the light of their new faith. 'Why not rather suffer injury?' (6:7) The ordinary quarrelsomeness of every human society becomes the opportunity to discover the endless self-sacrifice involved in Christian discipleship. Or again, the eucharist in Corinth was becoming bedevilled by differences of social class and wealth

(11:16-22). The matter could easily have been settled by some common-sense compromise. But no, Paul is inspired by it to probe deeper into the meaning of the eucharist itself, so that a trivial instance of human insensitivity becomes the occasion for an exploration into the mystery of the Lord's Supper. 'A man must test himself before eating his share of the bread and drinking the cup' (11:28) – thus a transient disorder in Corinth drew from Paul's pen a general observation which has served Christians as a guide-line of spiritual discipline ever since. And so it is again and again. Even the magisterial letter to the Romans was elicited by what were doubtless quite mundane sources of friction between Jews and Gentiles (e.g. 14:13-15). But such is the depth and scope of Paul's reply that his letter has been re-cognized ever since as offering an inimitable presentation of the central truths of the Christian faith.

Paul's letters, then, like all good letters, are intensely personal but at the same time are seldom trivial: they raise big issues and are not afraid to treat them on a grand scale. It was nothing new for professional writers in the ancient world to use the form of 'letters' to publish their ideas – indeed some of the philosophers, such as Epicurus, have left us little else. But such letters read like what they are: academic exercises, having only the form of a letter. After a few sentences the reader forgets that it is supposed to be a letter, and the occasional interjections of a more personal kind seem transparently artificial. Paul's letters, by contrast, bear the marks of a genuine correspondence. As we have seen, they were written in response to particular situations, and tackled specific issues that had arisen. They begin and end with the kind of greetings which are familiar from hundreds of letters, written in Greek on papyrus, which have been preserved in the sands of Egypt. Yet (unlike those letters) they are never stereotyped. Indeed the surprising thing, when one compares Paul's letters with those of his contemporaries, is how different they are. Even his letter to Philemon – a brief single-side affair concerning a very specific matter – though it is about the same length as most of the papyrus letters and begins and ends with similar formulas of greeting, nevertheless uses these conventional forms in a quite new way, so that the result, though still a perfectly correct letter, is also a timeless example of a man's passionate faith infusing every sentence he writes. And so it is with the longer epistles: real personal letters, starting out from the conventional forms, but transformed into a new kind of literature by the sheer genius of the writer.

Genius? Yes, most people would agree that Paul had genius. But can anyone ever keep it up all the time? Read first the warmly personal letter which Paul wrote to the church at Philippi, a letter which bears the mark of his personality as clearly as anything he wrote. But then go on to read Ephesians. We noticed in chapter 2 that the early part of this letter slips into the style and form of a prayer; does it not seem also that the personality of the writer begins to vanish behind these sonorous phrases, so that we can no longer feel instinctively that it is Paul who writes it? Add to this the fact that Ephesians, unlike the others letters seems to be addressed (apart from the opening greeting) to no one in particular and to be concerned with no particular topic: is it not more like a sermon which a travelling preacher might carry in his pocket than a message intended for a particular group of people at a particular moment? Of course Paul may have had his off-moments and have slipped into this more impersonal style from time to time; but it need not surprise us greatly that, for these and other reasons, scholars have cast doubts on the genuineness of Ephesians, and have suggested that it was written perhaps by some disciple or imitator of Paul. Then turn on to the so-called 'Pastoral' epistles – 1 and 2 Timothy and Titus. Here again the style is different: the old passionate argument and appeal seems to have turned into a manner that is distinctly schoolmasterly. Moreover, the situation seems to have changed: we no longer sense the excitement of new discoveries and new solutions in the dawn of a new faith, but rather the need to hold on, to consolidate, to concentrate on organization and rules. Of course these changes may have taken place, both in Paul himself and in his churches, during Paul's lifetime. But again it should not surprise us that a great many scholars now believe that the Pastorals were written by a later imitator who gave plausibility to his work by adding (or perhaps incorporating from some genuine but unpublished letter) the startlingly personal paragraphs which appear, for example, towards the end of 2 Timothy.

Imitator? Are we suggesting that the New Testament contains forgeries? Not exactly – for a forgery is intended to deceive, and there is no suggestion that this writer, whoever he was, was trying to deceive anyone. Rather we must imagine that, having lived perhaps very close to Paul, he was dutifully writing down what he sincerely believed Paul would have said had he been there – which was perhaps exactly what the church wanted to hear. The literary conventions of the time were less strict than ours about the names of authors being 'genuine'. No one would have been shocked to know that a letter, ostensibly by Paul, was in fact written by someone so steeped in Paul's thinking that he could be relied on to reproduce the mind of the master. Problems only arise in later centuries, when we, for reasons of our own, feel we need to know what is certainly by Paul himself and what is not.

So it is possible that the writings in the New Testament which go under the name of Paul include pages, or even whole letters, which are not directly from his hand. Perhaps too (as we have seen) Paul himself occasionally worked other things – such as an existing hymn or prayer – into his writing. In other words, we cannot always be sure that what we are reading is what came directly from Paul's own mind. Yet none of this greatly affects the impression made on us by his letters as a whole – the impression of a writer of extraordinary power, energy and originality. This writer also, incidentally, gave new life to the art of letter-writing itself, as well as formulating, in a way that has never been surpassed, some of the fundamental truths of the Christian faith.

PASSAGES FOR REFERENCE AND FURTHER STUDY

Autobiographical Galatians 1:13 – 2:1 (cp. Acts 9);
  2 Corinthians 1:8-11; 4:7-15; 11:21-33; Philippians 1:12-26;
  (?) 2 Timothy 4:6-18
Relationship with churches Romans 15:14-33; 2 Corinthians
  2:1-11; 6:11-13; Philippians 4:1-9
Practical issues transcended 1 Corinthians 6:1-11; 11:17-34;
  2 Corinthians 9; Philemon

9 The Emergence of the Gospels

By looking at some of the activities and concerns of the first Christian communities, and by listening in to the ways they tried to present their new faith to their non-Christian neighbours, we have begun to see why certain pages of the New Testament are as they are. They were written in response to particular needs and particular emergencies, and they yield their meaning to us only to the extent that we can enter into the situations which produced them. But we still have not given an account of the best-known parts of the New Testament and its longest consecutive writings: the Gospels. For what purpose or occasion were these narratives of the life of Jesus compiled, written as they were (according to the usual view) between thirty and sixty years after the events they describe? Moreover, why do we have four of them, three strangely like each other and one startlingly different? And what is the relationship between them?

To the first of these questions one would have thought that there would be a simple common-sense answer: the gospels were surely written because people wanted to know more about the life of Jesus and (as time passed) to have his teaching preserved in a reliable form. In broad terms this answer is more likely than any other to be correct. Nevertheless the facts turn out to be a good deal more complicated. In the first place, we have to reckon with the surprising observation that Paul in his letters seems to show virtually no interest in any of the sort of information about Jesus which is the subject of the gospels, and certainly makes no reference to any written account of Jesus' life. This takes us up to about twenty-five years after the crucifixion, at which time it was still apparently possible for a prominent church leader such as Paul to hold his faith, conduct his teaching and pursue his mission without the help of anything like a written gospel (and in fact this seems to be true also of the writers of virtually all the other New Testament letters). This does not mean, of course, that nothing whatever existed in Paul's lifetime which could have formed at least the basis of the gospels when in due course they came to be written down. On the contrary, detailed information about Jesus must have been preserved in people's memories, and even perhaps in writing, from the moment the church began its life after the resurrection; otherwise there could never have been any gospels at all. But it does mean that the emergence of the gospels was not quite so inevitable or so rapid as we might have thought, and that when we read them we must always remember that they were written at least a generation after the events they describe.

The second complicating factor follows on from the first. If there was such a long interval between the events of Jesus' life-time and the composition of the gospels, was it possible to write a consecutive 'life' at all? There were certain fixed points, of course: Jesus' birth and the beginning of his public ministry at one end, his trial, death and resurrection at the other. But what of the events in between? Most of the material which fills the gospels consists of self-contained episodes and short snatches of teaching – things which do not have to be in any particular order. It is true that we find most of these incidents in much the same order in the first three gospels – but then, as we shall see in a moment, they have probably deliberately followed each other's arrangement. Moreover, even in these three gospels quite a number of passages occur at different stages in Jesus' life and work: compare for instance the place of the sayings about John the Baptist in Matthew (11:2-19) and Luke (7:18-35). And when we turn to the fourth gospel, even an episode as important as the 'cleansing of the temple' stands in a totally different place in the story (John 2:14-16; compare Mark 11:15-17).

This point too can be taken a good deal further. Consider Jesus' saying, 'You shall sit on twelve thrones judging the twelve tribes of Israel'. In Matthew, this occurs in the course of a discussion about discipleship in general, and in response to a question from Jesus' closest followers about their own personal reward (19:28). In Luke, on the other hand, it comes in the middle of Jesus' discourse at the last supper (22:30). That is to say, it looks as though, at first, the saying itself was remembered but not the circumstances which caused Jesus to utter it. And this, after all, is hardly surprising. Jesus' sayings are mostly very pointed and memorable, and will have remained vividly in people's memories. But what Jesus was doing when he gave any particular piece of teaching, or exactly whereabouts he was when he performed a certain cure, are the kind of facts which will have been easily and quickly forgotten. We must face the possibility that virtually all the information which came the way of the first gospel-writer was of this disconnected kind, and that, to make a consecutive narrative at all, he was faced with the the task of piecing it together as best he could. Add to this the fact that (as we have seen) quite a number of these episodes were remembered, not just because they said something about Jesus, but because they helped the church to cope with problems that had arisen after the resurrection, and had even perhaps been somewhat altered in the process. It follows that the actual evolution of the gospels as we know them today must have been something much more complicated than the mere putting together of material for a 'life' of Jesus.

It was this last point which gave rise, some fifty years ago, to what has turned out to be one of the most influential ideas which have ever been brought to bear on the study of the New Testament: 'Form-criticism'. It was realized that if one were to understand at all what had been going on between the resurrection and the emergence of the gospels one would have to stop reading the gospels as consecutive narratives and divide them up instead into all the originally separate units out of which they must have been composed. These units (for which a Greek technical term was used: *pericopē*) could then be reshuffled according to their 'form': one could gather the healing stories into one pile, the exorcisms into another, the argumentative sayings into another, the exhortations into another and so forth. And one could then ask what needs and problems and challenges in the early church caused these different units to be remembered and then to be recorded in the 'forms' in which we have them. We have already seen how this process may have been at work in a small way in certain parts of the New Testament. 'Form-criticism' is the systematic application of the idea to the whole of the material in the gospels.

For our present purpose, all this has one implication of great importance. When we read a biography today, one of the things we expect to learn about the hero is his *development*. We expect the writer to show how his subject's ideas changed over the years, how his personality came to maturity, how his gifts and abilities were adapted to changing circumstances. Only so do we feel that we can get to know the real person; only so does his inner nature reveal itself to us. But we have just seen that in the case of Jesus we cannot be sure what order things happened in, and so we simply do not have the material for building up a picture of his life and development. Earlier studies of the life of Jesus used to talk of his *gradual* acceptance of his mission, his *growing* realization of his Messiahship, and so forth. Today we realize that we cannot say anything of this kind. In this sense, the gospels are not 'biographies' at all. But at the same time we can perhaps see better than we could in the past what they *are*, and that in their own way they do tell us things about Jesus which it is vitally important that we should know. More will be said about this when we come to look at each of the gospels in turn.

But before we can do that we must face the other question with which we began. Why four gospels anyway? And how are they related to each other? In antiquity these questions did not seem very important. It was as natural and providential, people thought, that there should be four gospels as that there should be four points of the compass, and the scraps of historical information about the four evangelists which have come down to us are so confused that they really do not help us at all (a second-century authority tells us, for instance, that Matthew's gospel was originally written in Hebrew; but any competent linguistic scholar can tell, by reading the Greek text, that it is certainly not a translation of a Hebrew original). So we have very little to guide us. We stand before these four short compositions and simply have to work out for ourselves the answers to our questions.

Let us first set down the points on which everyone would agree. First, it is obvious that Matthew, Mark and Luke are very closely related to each other, whereas John stands apart on its own. Our question, therefore, is not so much why there are four gospels, but why there are three such similar gospels (and here again a Greek technical term is used to mean 'similar in scope': *synoptic*). Secondly, there are passages in the synoptic gospels which are almost identical, so much so that the resemblance can hardly be explained as a common recollection of the same story. No, when two or even three gospels use so many of the same words and idioms when narrating the same episodes, far the most probable explanation is that one gospel writer copied from another. But thirdly, there are also some passages where the synoptic gospels differ quite sharply from each other, or leave things out, or put new things in. In other words, if they copied from each other, they also often departed from each other; and of this phenomenon too there are several different variations. Sometimes each of the three versions goes its own way; sometimes two agree and the third is different. In other words, the *'synoptic problem'* comes down to this: how are we to explain that we have three separate writings which show *both* close similarities *and* striking differences between each other?

Strictly speaking, the problem is insoluble. The gospels themselves do not give us the answers we are looking for, and there is nowhere else we can look. All we can do is think out some possible combinations, try them out and see which works best. We can start with a simple clue. Mark's gospel is the shortest and contains virtually nothing which does not occur in Matthew. Either, then, Mark is simply an abbreviated version of Matthew (which was the usual view for many centuries) or else it was the first to be written and was then expanded by Matthew – in which case Luke probably used Mark also, though in a slightly less slavish way. For various reasons this second explanation is now usually held to work better. But unfortunately we cannot go on from there to say simply that Matthew and Luke each enlarged and improved on Mark in their own way. For there are certain passages which occur in almost identical form in Matthew and Luke but which are absent altogether from Mark. It is possible that Luke had in front of him both Mark and Matthew (or, if Luke was written before Matthew, that Matthew had both Mark and Luke). But this would have made his task extraordinarily complicated. The alternative is to assume that there once existed some other document which was used by both Matthew and Luke to supplement what they found in Mark. If it ever existed, this document – for which scholars have used the symbol 'Q' – must have consisted mainly of Jesus' teaching, since there is very little else on which Matthew and Luke agree when they are not following Mark.

This, in broad outline, is the explanation of these puzzling facts which has been most popular for the last fifty years or so: Mark was written first; Matthew and Luke used Mark (and followed the chronological outline of his narrative) but used also another document, 'Q', to which they both had access. It has been most popular, not because it can be proved true, but simply because it appears to work better – to explain more facts – than any other hypothesis. We need to start somewhere: and this theory at least provides us with a starting-point. If we find it is fruitful we may decide to stick to it, and we may even come to be convinced by it. But we must never forget that no one knows, and no one ever can know, for certain. Today some scholars are beginning once again to play seriously with other possible combinations. And if any of my readers wish to try their hand at working out another hypothesis which explains more satisfactorily the puzzling relationship of the first three gospels, let them get to work at once!

10 Mark

Mark's gospel is the shortest. It is also the most austere, the least polished – almost uncouth, in fact – compared with the others. All of which makes it still more probable that it is the earliest – for we can imagine Matthew and Luke improving on Mark's style and presentation, but it would have been odd for Mark to have deliberately taken the polish off what he found, say, in Matthew. And if Mark is both the earliest and the simplest account we have, then it would seem to follow that it is in Mark that we should look for the most direct and authentic portrait of Jesus.

This, in fact, is precisely what scholars have been doing for the last hundred years or so. If we accept the hypothesis that both Matthew and Luke actually had Mark in front of them when they wrote their own gospels – and we have seen that this does seem in many ways the most probable explanation of their relationship – then we can immediately start on some detective work. We can look at episodes which are recorded by both Mark and (shall we say) Matthew, and we can note the small alterations which Matthew has made. We can then do the same with all the passages which appear in both gospels, and by putting together and sorting out all Matthew's alterations we can begin to get some impression of what sort of editor Matthew was – what he regarded as particularly important about Jesus, what aspects of his teaching needed to be emphasized and so forth. In other words, the personality and interests of the author of this gospel begin to come alive to us, and we feel we can glimpse at least some of the reasons why he painted the portrait of Jesus as he did (this fascinating study has gained among experts the rather forbidding technical name of 'Redaction criticism').

But what then of Mark? The natural result of thinking of Matthew and Luke as 'editors' of what they found in Mark is that we begin to regard Mark as a more impersonal and objective record – rather like a photograph compared with the more subjective portraits of the other two evangelists. At first reading, there are many features of Mark's gospel which seem to confirm this impression. The narrative begins abruptly, and introduces Jesus as already fully adult approaching John the Baptist for his own baptism – no place here for those narratives of Jesus' birth and infancy which give Luke in particular a chance to display his wonderful powers of narrative and description. Then again, in the episode of the 'Temptation', Mark is satisfied with a bare sentence of factual reporting (1:12-13), leaving it to his 'editors' to fill in the details (from whatever source they had them) of Jesus' encounter with Satan. And so on right through the gospel: very little account of the teaching of Jesus, very little elaboration. The story moves quickly towards the final week in Jerusalem, the point at which the three accounts come very close together. We may feel that here we have the basic facts about Jesus, presented as plainly and objectively as we could wish.

But on a second reading doubts may begin to arise. Note, for example, Jesus' strangely reiterated insistence that those around him — and indeed the demons also – should keep his true identity secret. If you look at the same episodes as recorded in Matthew and Luke, you find the same motif, certainly, but much less frequently. You may say that the 'editors' either did not like or else even did not understand what Mark was getting at when he recorded these injunctions to secrecy. But was Mark 'getting at' something? A moment ago we were thinking of him as one who simply set down the facts as they happened. Are we now to imagine him as a writer who also imposed his own interpretation?

This particular instance – which scholars have come to call the problem of the 'Messianic Secret' – has caused this question to be asked more insistently than any other feature of Mark's gospel. Suppose, for example, that as a matter of historical fact it was only after the resurrection that anyone began to think of Jesus as the 'Messiah' at all. This would have placed the evangelist in a difficulty. Surely (he would have felt) Jesus' miracles and personality were such as to make at least some people guess his true identity during his lifetime. And his answer would have been (it is suggested) that the reason why Jesus was not generally recognized must have been because he explicitly and sternly told those who did guess his 'secret' not to divulge it to anyone. This explanation is perhaps too ingenious, and in any case can be shown not to fit all the facts. But for our present purpose the solution of the problem is not the most important thing. The significant point gained is that the problem exists, and that therefore it does look as if Mark, far from presenting a completely neutral account, in fact 'edited' his sources just as the others did.

Indeed there are other instances that point the same way. Mark records a fair number of Jesus' miracles, and it is clear that there were many more which he might have mentioned (1:33-4). But Jesus was by no means the only holy man of his time who performed such feats. We hear of others who had built up a similar reputation. Yet Jesus was far more than just another miracle-worker. The gospel was written precisely to show how different he was – indeed it was written to show that he was unique, the Son of God. And so the miracles must have been more than just ordinary cures and exorcisms. Sure enough, we find that again and again the author of this gospel works in some reference to 'faith': Jesus' miracles are told as illustrations of the importance of faith in the relationship between man and God. We can hardly be wrong if we see, here again, a deliberate touch of the evangelist, exercising his subtle skill as an editor to convey the interpretation he felt the facts demanded.

We have already seen that certain passages in the gospels, as in other parts of the New Testament, can best be understood in the light of debates going on at the time they were written. In the early years there was certainly controversy between the Christians and the Jews (out of whose society most of the Christians had come). One of the matters over which controversy inevitably came to a head was that of the continuing validity of the Jewish food laws. As we saw, an episode was recalled which seemed relevant to the dispute, and was recorded in such a way in Mark's gospel that the church could see at once how Jesus' teaching settled the question for them (see above, page 30). But there were broader questions at issue than this. What, ultimately, was the difference between the Jewish religion and Christianity? In the long run, perhaps, it was not very great. 'Do you believe the prophets?' asked Paul of King Agrippa (Acts 26:27), with the clear implication that it was but a short step from there to accepting the Christian faith. But of course it would depend on what sort of Judaism you were thinking of. In Jerusalem, the main emphasis for many Jews was naturally on the Temple, with its daily sacrifices, its festivals, its rules of ritual purity and its exclusion of all but Jews from its inner precincts. That sort of religion was obviously a far cry from the universal spiritual values proclaimed by Christianity. But if one thinks of the kind of religion practised, say, by a Greek-speaking Jew in the city of Rome, the picture is very different. Such a man went regularly to the synagogue every sabbath, listened to readings from the Law of Moses, heard sermons exhorting him to live accordingly, and in short was schooled to be a faithful adherent of what was widely regarded as the most exalted and ethically demanding monotheistic religion then known in the world. How different was this from the new cult of Christianity?

With this question in mind, read the following conversation in Mark's gospel:

> Then one of the lawyers, who had been listening to these discussions and had noted how well he answered, came forward and asked him, 'Which commandment is first of all?' Jesus answered, 'The first is, "Hear, O Israel: the Lord our God is the only Lord; love the Lord your God with all your heart, with all your soul, with all your mind, and with all your strength." The second is this: "Love your neighbour as yourself." There is no other commandment greater than these.' The lawyer said to him, 'Well said, Master. You are right in saying that God is one and beside him there is no other. And to love him with all your heart, all your understanding, and all your strength, and to love your neighbour as yourself – that is far more than any burnt offerings or sacrifices.' When Jesus saw how sensibly he answered, he said to him, 'You are not far from the kingdom of God.'
>
> (Mark 12:28-34 NEB)

'You are not far from the kingdom of God.' Can we doubt that this was precisely the answer the Christian community yearned to give to their Jewish neighbours? The gap was so small – if only the Jews would cross it!

Thus we are beginning to see in Mark, as we shall see in Matthew and Luke, not just an impersonal scribe compiling and recording all that could be remembered about the life of Jesus, but a writer with a mind of his own who selected from the material available to him the episodes and sayings which he knew would be of most interest and concern to his readers, and presented them in such a way that they offered not just a record but an interpretation of the life and work of Jesus. But at this point we can hardly remain content with regarding him simply as the shadowy figure who happened to write the gospel. We want to know who this 'Mark' was, and where and when he wrote. Are any answers available to these questions?

On the whole, Christian writers of the second century onwards seem to have known very little about the authors of the gospels and the circumstances in which they wrote. But in the case of Mark we are given rather more information: a number of ancient writers agree that he was indeed the 'John Mark' mentioned in Acts and certain letters of Paul, and that he wrote his gospel in Rome on the basis of recollections supplied to him by Peter. This sounds to us now a little too simple: we have been finding reason to think of Mark's work as a good deal more subtle and sophisticated than merely taking down the reminiscences of an older apostle. But in outline there is no reason why the tradition should not be correct; and the connection with Rome is confirmed and illuminated by one very striking detail. Introducing Simon of Cyrene, who carried Jesus' cross, Mark mentions that he was the 'father of Alexander and Rufus' (15:21). This should make us pause; for there could have been no point in such a reference unless the first readers (or hearers) of the gospel knew these two brothers personally! That is to say, the congregation for whom Mark wrote included the sons of one of the actors in the drama – who would certainly have protested had Mark got anything seriously wrong! By this chance reference we are given unexpected confirmation of the general reliability of the gospel; and when we find Paul writing to the Romans and greeting a certain Rufus in that city (16:13) it is hard to resist the conclusion that this is the same son of Simon of Cyrene, and that Mark's gospel, therefore, was originally intended for the church at Rome.

But there is still one very puzzling matter to be mentioned. According to the oldest manuscripts the gospel breaks off with the words, 'for they were afraid' (16:8). Other manuscripts do offer an ending – or rather two alternative endings – but these have almost certainly been added by a later hand. We say 'breaks off', but of course this is a modern judgement. We have our own ideas about how a book should end, and this certainly does not look like an ending. Yet we cannot be certain that its first readers would have felt the same – indeed it is quite possible, with a little ingenuity, to think of reasons why Mark may have actually intended his gospel to end at that point. But it remains odd, to say the least, that the narrative should stop short of what in the other gospels is the climax – the resurrection – and should leave us with nothing but the fear and bewilderment of the women at the tomb. It may be preferable, therefore, to imagine that Mark for some reason was not able to finish his gospel, or that the end of the scroll got torn off – all of which, of course, is pure speculation. The mystery remains – a fitting reminder, perhaps, that though we may feel that we have begun to lay bare some of Mark's secrets, his little book contains far more mysteries than we shall ever be able to give an account of, and will continue to keep its readers fascinated and even a little mystified for as long as it continues to be read at all.

PASSAGES FOR REFERENCE AND FURTHER STUDY

References to 'John Mark'   Acts 12:12, 25; 15:37-39;
   2 Timothy 4:11; (?) Colossians 4:10; 1 Peter 5:13
'Secrecy' passages   Mark 1:34; 1:44; 3:12; 5:43; 7:36; 8:26
Faith and miracles   Mark 2:1-5; 4:35-41; 5:36; 9:14-29;
   10:46-52; 11:20-24

11 Matthew

'It was said . . . but I say unto you . . .' Every teacher, at one time or another, has to measure himself against those who have gone before him and define his own position in relation to theirs. Jesus was no exception; and all the gospels reveal him as one ready to revise traditional teaching and to attack the views and attitudes of other religious leaders and teachers. Yet it remains true that it is in Matthew's gospel that this note of controversy becomes particularly strident. It occurs in the Sermon on the Mount, with its radical modifications of what was 'said of old time', its sarcastic attacks on the Pharisees for 'blowing their own trumpet', and even its scornful look at Gentiles with their wordy prayers (6:7); it occurs in numerous attacks on the Pharisees and Scribes for both their doctrine and their conduct; it occurs in arguments with the Sadducees and High Priests – in short, to a degree greater than anywhere else in the New Testament, Jesus appears as a highly controversial figure.

Now there is no doubt that Jesus *was* a controversial figure. Yet we can hardly be wrong (particularly if we follow the clues we have found elsewhere in the New Testament) if we pick up a hint in the accounts of the controversies surrounding Jesus that somewhat similar controversies were in progress when the gospel came to be written. When we read the accounts of the arguments which raged around Jesus, we can surely overhear the arguments which raged around the early Christians. In Matthew, traces of such arguments are particularly easy to find. Consider a turn of phrase like this:

> 'They will deliver you up to councils, and flog you in their synagogues' (10:17 in RSV, which is here closer to the original Greek than NEB).

Why 'their' synagogues? We would have expected simply 'the' synagogues. Surely the Christian church on one side stood over against the Jewish establishment on the other, with all its apparatus of temple, synagogues, priests and rabbis. But no – *their* synagogues. We must look at another possibility. Was this church perhaps composed entirely or almost entirely of Jews, who continued to have many of the same institutions and practices – even 'synagogues' of their own – but were involved in controversy all the more bitter with official Judaism precisely because, in certain respects, they had broken away and begun to make their own rules? Did the Christians think of their own communities as 'our' synagogues over against 'their' synagogues?

Once we begin to imagine a church of this kind, all sorts of phrases in Matthew's gospel spring to life. On the one hand, the Christians are not going to be outdone by the Jewish community in respect of moral behaviour and strict adherence to the law (at least as Jesus had interpreted it). Did not Jesus say, 'I did not come to destroy the law . . .' (5:17), 'one jot or one tittle shall not pass away from the law . . .' (5:18), 'unless your righteousness exceeds that of the Scribes and Pharisees . . .' (5:20)? But at the same time they must be different! Jesus also said, 'Do and keep all that they say, but do not copy their deeds' (23:3). 'They love to be called by men Rabbi, but you must not be called Rabbi' (23:7-8). Or again, the organization of the Christian 'synagogue' will be very like that of the Jewish synagogue – an erring brother must be tried on the evidence of two or three witnesses, as laid down in the Old Testament (18:16). But it will also be different; for what community of Jews ever showed such patience with an offender or gave him as many chances as the Christians did, given Jesus' radical command to forgive seventy times seven times (18:21-22)? Yet even for Christians there must sometimes be a limit; and they used a typically Jewish phrase to express the fact that they could no longer admit someone to their assemblies – he would be on the same footing as a Gentile or a tax collector! (18:17)

All this adds up to a kind of love–hate relationship with the Jewish community which is unique in the New Testament. The Christians (as many of them as were Jews by race, which must have been the great majority in this church) evidently felt themselves to be still Jews also by religion and culture. Yet they were no longer (if they ever had been) simply a sect within Judaism, a group who held different views on certain matters but who otherwise continued to form part of Jewish society. On the contrary, there was now keen argument, if not enmity, between the two 'synagogues', and the Christians had both to defend themselves against Jewish attacks (for example, with regard to their respect for the Law of Moses or their attitude to traditional sabbath regulations) and at the same time to show reason for their departure from many aspects of official Jewish teaching. It is this tense and sometimes angry situation which again and again explains the way in which Matthew's gospel selects and arranges the sayings and activities of Jesus.

What were the matters in dispute? We have seen how at Antioch the point at issue between Christians and Jews was the strict observance of the Jewish food laws. But the debate could also be conducted along more general lines. Behind every particular dispute lay the ultimate question: did or did not the Christians regard the Law of Moses (as the Jews did) as their ultimate authority, or did they now reject it in favour of the new authority of Christ (in which case they could no longer claim any common ground with the Jews at all)? Sooner or later the Jewish Christians would have to make up their minds about their attitude to the Law; and Matthew's gospel was clearly intended to present Jesus' teaching in a way that would help them to do so.

For here perhaps is the most striking difference of all between Mark and Matthew. Mark's gospel contains astonishingly little teaching. If one asks, what did Jesus actually *say*, one receives no answer (except for the barest summaries) until one reaches the parable of the Sower and its interpretation in chapter 4; and thereafter the only discourse of any length is Jesus' series of pronouncements about the future in chapter 13. How different is the presentation in Matthew's gospel! The reader who is interested to know what Jesus taught has only to wait until the preliminaries are over – Jesus' birth, his baptism, the temptation and the call of the first disciples – and then he is given the longest piece of Jesus' teaching that occurs anywhere in the synoptic gospels: the Sermon on the Mount (chapters 5-7). Nor is that all. Besides reproducing – and indeed adding to – the discourses which Mark does include (the parable chapter and the discourse on the future – in Matthew, chapters 13 and 24), Matthew gives us two new ones – the missionary charge to the apostles in chapter 10 (of which there are only seven verses in Mark) and

the chapter on the discipline and organization of the church
(ch. 18) – seven chapters of consecutive teaching compared with
only two in Mark.

This emphasis on Jesus' teaching is confirmed by some significant details. If Jesus is intended to come over so strongly as a
teacher, then we may expect that his followers will have to
acquit themselves as *learners*. And this, again, is exactly what we
find. In Mark, the disciples, by any reckoning, make a poor
showing. Not only do they desert Jesus at the end, but they
constantly fail to understand what he is saying and doing, and
are reprimanded accordingly. Of course they fail too in Matthew.
But significantly, where in Mark their failure is in understanding,
in Matthew it is always in *faith;* for however disappointing they
may be in other respects, at least they are always good learners
and intelligent pupils. Indeed their task is explicitly summed up
at the end of the gospel in these terms: they are to teach men to
'keep all the commandments I gave you' (28:20). Matthew's
gospel emphasizes with unique insistence the magisterial teaching
of Jesus and the importance of his hearers correctly handing on
that teaching to others.

There is one more feature to notice of the way Matthew
presents Jesus' teaching. The long consecutive discourses can
be set out as follows:

The Sermon on the Mount (chapters 5-7)
The Missionary Charge (chapter 10)
The parable-discourse (chapter 13)
The discourse on church order (chapter 18)
The discourse on the future (chapter 24)

Five discourses in all. But the Law of Moses was also presented
in five parts – the so-called 'Pentateuch' (the first five books of
the Bible). And did not Jesus proclaim God's law from a 'mount',
just as Moses did from Mount Sinai? In other ways too there
seem to be deliberate points of comparison: Jesus, like Moses,
was 'called out of Egypt' (2:15); like Moses, he was forty
days in the wilderness (4:2; compare Exodus 34:28). Was
Jesus then a new Moses? Was this how the question of the Law
could now be answered: Jesus was indeed a new legislator, but

one who built securely on the foundation laid by Moses?

The comparison must not be pressed too far. Jesus is not only a 'new Moses', he is at times also a new Elijah, a new prophet, a new David. The evangelist may not have meant his hints to be taken too literally. Yet there can be no doubt that the question of the authority of Jesus' teaching, over against that of the Law of Moses (which for any Jew, after all, was the Law of God) is a question which was never far from the mind of the author of this gospel, and which must therefore have been of particular concern to the church or churches for whom he wrote. Can we, in conclusion, say anything more about his first hearers and readers? Can we overhear any of the conversations going on in 'Matthew's church'?

We have noted that one of the long discourses in Matthew – which we have called the 'Missionary Charge' to the disciples (chapter 10) – is an expansion of what in Mark amounts to only seven verses (3:13-19). But when we ask where Matthew found all the other material for this chapter, we find to our surprise that much of it comes from other parts of Mark, particularly the discourse on the future (Mark 13), which was intended to give hope and encouragement to the disciples in the face of impending tribulation. In other words, Matthew has clearly introduced into his 'mission' chapter sayings which originally belonged to another context, and has thereby compiled a kind of manual for the Christians of his time to use when they faced perplexity and discouragement in their efforts to bring the gospel to others.

If then we take this 'manual' as a whole, we can get some idea of what these Christians' circumstances were. 'Do not take the road into gentile lands!' is the command of Jesus put right at the beginning (10:5). But if anything is certain, it is that by the time this was written down in the gospel the Christian mission had gone deep into gentile lands, and had been spectacularly successful. Why then is this curiously restrictive saying of Jesus given such prominence? Perhaps we may find a clue in another saying a few verses later. 'You will not have got through all the cities of Israel, before the Son of Man comes' (10:23). The Christians had been hammering away at their Jewish neighbours for a whole generation. The task seemed hopeless: the Jewish synagogue showed no sign of softening in its attitude, the Jews' antagonism was becoming if anything stronger, and their conversion seemed out of the question. Meanwhile, in other parts of the world, the mission to the Gentiles was going from strength to strength. Why should not these beleaguered Jewish Christians give up the unequal struggle to convert their fellow-Jews and seek out sympathetic Gentiles instead? But no, their evangelist brought them sternly back to their primary task. Were not Jesus' own priorities absolutely clear – first the Jews, and only then the Gentiles? 'Do not take the road into gentile lands . . .'

Perhaps this reconstruction takes us further than the evidence strictly allows. The precise stages of the missionary work of this part of the church can never be known to us. But that it was a church for which the 'Jewish question' was a dominant concern is beyond doubt; and Matthew's gospel was a way of presenting Jesus' life and work so as to give most help to those caught up in the fundamental issue of the Old and the New Israel.

PASSAGES FOR REFERENCE AND FURTHER STUDY

'Five Discourses'   chapters 5–7, 10, 13, 18 and 24
Controversy   chapter 23
Role of the disciples   13:52; 28:19–20

12 *Luke*

The Gospel and Acts

'Tell it the way it happened!' Virtually all the hints we have picked up so far about the methods and purposes of the gospel-writers have suggested that this was *not* what they primarily set out to do. They did not put down all they knew, they did not try to get everything arranged in the order in which it was actually done or spoken. But now look at the opening of Luke's gospel:

> . . . it seemed good to me also, having followed all things closely for some time past, to write an orderly account for you, most excellent Theophilus . . .

Certainly Luke sets out to write history more deliberately and self-consciously than any other New Testament writer, and this introduction (which is picked up again at the beginning of Acts) shows that he knew something about the rules and conventions of the writer's trade (see above, page 2). Yet when we read his gospel we do not find that it is so very different in style and presentation from Mark and Matthew. Certainly there are things about it which are distinctive and which one can soon learn to recognize as characteristically 'Lucan'. But no one could say that it is obviously much more 'historical' than the others. In which case it would seem to follow, either that we have been wrong about Mark and Matthew, or else that Luke's introduction gives a promise which is not altogether fulfilled.

This can be tested against the very first pages of the gospel – the 'infancy narratives', as scholars call the accounts of the birth and early childhood of John the Baptist and Jesus. Here Luke gives us something which is not in any of the other gospels (though there is a small overlap with the first two chapters of Matthew). He has also given us one of the most exquisite pieces of writing in the Bible, if not in the whole of literature, and one that has inspired countless works of art. But would it be right to call it *history*? The story is peopled with angels, punctuated by super-natural occurrences, enriched with poetry and adorned with all the resources of the story-teller's art. One need not necessarily deny that things may have actually happened like this (though it is fashionable for scholars to treat these pages as legend or at least as the fruit of pious meditation). But at the same time one must admit that these stories would have lost much of their power if they had been told *merely* as history, without the artistry and flair for detail which the author has brought to them. Add to this the fact that they are deliberately written in a distinctly Old Testament style, and that the events themselves recall episodes from the Old Testament (compare Mary's song (the Magnificat) with Hannah's hymn of joy in 1 Samuel 2). Luke's manner here is what literary critics would call pastiche: the story acquires a timeless quality from being told in the hallowed phrases of sacred history (and Luke read the Old Testament in a Greek translation, so that we can see quite easily where it has influenced his own Greek style).

But does all this add up to *history*? Luke gives no apology for the fact that, apart from one brief episode of Jesus' boyhood (2:41-51), he jumps straight from Jesus' infancy to his appearance beside the Jordan aged 'about thirty' (3:23) – his promise to write an 'orderly' account seems already to be belied. Yet at the same time a serious historical purpose does appear. At the beginning of chapter 3 there is an elaborate exercise in dating, which relates the events described not only to the reigns of the Roman emperor and of several subject rulers but also to the High Priests in office; and if one takes Acts (the second volume of his work) into view, there is a more deliberate effort to place the sequence of events in the context of world history than can be seen anywhere else in the New Testament. In other words, history is certainly *one* of the interests which Luke brought to his work. But it is not the only one. Indeed, one of the fascinations of studying Luke's work is discovering the many different styles in which he could write and the various different objects he had in writing.

Most of the New Testament writers were addressing themselves to readers who already knew quite a lot about Jesus and about their faith. But there are signs that Luke was anxious to get his book read by a wider public – people like Theophilus – and that he gave some thought to ways of making things easier for them to understand. How, for example, was someone who was not familiar with the culture of Palestine to try to imagine Jesus? As a teacher, an exorcist, a philosopher? It looks as though Luke deliberately arranged his material so as to suggest an answer. There is a long section of his gospel (9:51 – 19:28) which describes Jesus' journey from Galilee to Jerusalem. There is of course no doubt that Jesus made such a journey – all the gospels mention it, and in Mark and Matthew it marks a significant transition from the popular successes of Jesus' work in Galilee to his passion and death in Jerusalem. But in Luke the journey, which would normally have taken at most two or three days on foot, is filled out with a large number of incidents, so much so that the reader has some trouble in keeping a clear picture in his mind of where Jesus is supposed to have got to at any particular moment. Luke, in fact, has used this journey as a framework into which to fit a large number of miscellaneous instances of Jesus' work and teaching. Why has he done this? Partly, no doubt, because this was a convenient solution of the problem where to put his extra material; but partly also because one of the stock figures with which his more sophisticated readers would have been familiar was that of the wandering preacher and teacher, the man constantly on the road, moving from place to place and attracting crowds by his teaching – there were many such in the ancient world. If you want to know what Jesus was like, Luke is saying, start with that picture in your mind – though of course Jesus was also much more than this, and you will have to combine this with other pictures as you go along.

Just such another picture occurs in what, to a practising Christian, is a most unexpected place. Jesus, we know, had 'disciples'. What was his relationship with them? Matthew, as we saw, exploits the Jewish model of a Rabbi with his pupils; and the same model of a respected teacher would have been intelligible also to a Hellenistic reader, who would have been familiar with philosophers who attracted a 'school' of disciples. Yet this was not the whole story. Jesus' followers were not merely 'learners'; they were also the men (as Luke was to go on to show in his second volume) who were to lead the new Christian movement after the resurrection. They must therefore have enjoyed Jesus'

trust and confidence, and have had an intimate share in his thinking and aspirations. How could this be brought vividly to mind?
Here, another historian's convention suggested itself. The great
leader, the night before some crisis or turning-point (a decisive
battle, for example), would gather his closest friends around him,
perhaps for a farewell meal together, and share with them his
hopes for the future and the ideals which he would wish to
see pursued by them in the event of his death. The history of
such a man, in other words, would include a scene of serious
and revealing 'table talk' on the eve of the crisis. But Jesus, as
everyone knew, certainly shared a meal with his disciples 'on
the night when he was betrayed'. The interest of Christians,
since very early times, has focused upon this meal as the institution
of an act of worship – the Lord's Supper or Eucharist. Luke's
narrative allows for this (though in detail it presents something
rather different from what we would regard as a standard
version of the institution). But if we try to read it without
thinking all the time of the Eucharist, we shall see that it was
not the details of the meal itself which interested Luke so much
as the things which were said at it. For (to our surprise) some of
Jesus' conversation with his disciples, which occurs in other
contexts in Mark and Matthew, is put in at this point. But we
can now guess why: Luke is following the convention that the
hero discloses his deepest thoughts to his friends on the eve of
the decisive day of his life. He is giving us Jesus' 'table talk',
and thereby adding to the picture of the itinerant teacher the
further picture of the leader surrounded by his closest friends
and associates and preparing them for the leadership of his movement after his death.

All this suggests that, even for Luke, the business of writing a
gospel involved something more serious and complex than
simply 'telling it the way it happened'. He too, like Mark and
Matthew, had to select, rearrange and edit his material so as to
help his readers (whom we may guess to have been somewhat
more cosmopolitan and sophisticated people than those for whom
the other two synoptic gospels were written) to understand and
appreciate the significance of Jesus of Nazareth. And indeed,
once one has begun, it is not difficult to identify other areas
where Luke has left his mark on the record. For example:

— he clearly set great store by Jesus' parable-teaching, and included many more parables than the other evangelists, as well as some of the best known and best loved (the Good Samaritan, the Prodigal Son, the Pharisee and the Publican);

— he was particularly well informed on local matters, and was able to get such things as the priestly rota at the temple (1:8-10) exactly right;

— he was struck by Jesus' open and generous attitude towards women (not at all typical of his time and culture) and gave numerous instances of it;

— he believed that Jesus had particularly important and challenging things to say about poverty and materialism;

— he was interested in the experience and work of the Holy Spirit, and allowed this interest to show through parts of the narrative.

Any reader can add to this list for himself after a careful reading of the gospel.

But there is one respect in which Luke is totally unlike any of the other gospel-writers. He is the only one of them to have followed his gospel with a second volume devoted to the history of the early church – a book which has been known since very early times as 'Acts of the Apostles'. This title is not entirely apt. It was probably given to the work because there existed a literary *genre* known as 'Acts' of famous people. But in fact only two apostles have any prominence in it, Peter and Paul; and a better description of the book would be a 'History' of the early years of the church. For once again there can be no doubt that Luke was intending to write serious history. He took considerable trouble to place the events of his narrative in their wider historical context; his references to Roman officials and institutions are circumstantial and usually correct; and he was well aware of the conventions within which other historians worked, such as the need to insert speeches by the principal characters in order to bring out the significance of events. (How far Luke possessed records of what Peter and Paul may have said on particular occasions is a disputed question; but it was certainly Luke who summarized and edited their speeches and sermons and who used his literary skill to work them into his history.)

Yet – as with all good history-writing – we shall appreciate Acts more if we look in it, not just for a factual account of what took place, but for a deliberate selection and presentation of those facts in order to document the writer's own convictions. Again, we need only refer to some of the questions at issue:

— did the Christian church constitute a threat to the Roman authorities? Luke's accounts of the various civil disturbances in which Paul and others were involved were clearly meant to demonstrate that in each case there was not and could not have been any question of disobedience towards the Roman authorities;

— was the expansion of the church haphazard and dangerously disorganized? Luke's narrative constitutes an argument that it was from the first under the control and guidance of the Holy Spirit, and that its founder members were always in agreement over essentials;

— did new Christian centres spring up mushroom-like, without plan or co-ordination? Luke is always able to show how each new branch of the church was founded and authorized ultimately from Jerusalem;

— is the long sequence of events which in the end brought Paul as a prisoner to Rome to be seen as a series of vicissitudes hindering the missionary work of the church? On the contrary, in Luke's presentation it demonstrates the triumphant progress of the gospel from Jerusalem to the very heart of the pagan world, where Paul, though held on remand under house-arrest for two years, was able to 'proclaim the Kingdom of God and give teaching about the Lord Jesus Christ quite freely and without constraint' (28:31).

Again, the attentive reader will be able to make his own additions to this list. But perhaps the most significant point of all is this: that almost alone of the New Testament writers Luke is speaking to *us*, his readers. Elsewhere, it is usually as if we are overhearing a conversation that was not originally intended for our ears. But Luke is writing for people outside the charmed circle, and he uses the resources of a historian, a story-teller, a poet and many others in order to get his meaning over to anyone who may chance to pick up his work. The idioms and conventions he uses belong of course not to our world but his: we have to learn to appreciate his style and his editoral technique before we can hear what he wants to tell us. But when we have done so, we shall find a directness and immediacy in Luke's writings which make us go back to them again and again if we wish to be personally touched and challenged by the record of Jesus and the early church.

PASSAGES FOR REFERENCE AND FURTHER STUDY

Literary form
- (a) Dedications   Luke 1:1-4; Acts 1:1
- (b) Travel narrative   Luke 9:51–19:27
- (c) 'Table talk'   Luke 22:24-38

Special interests
- (a) Historical references   Luke 3:1-2; 23:7-12; Acts 11:27-30; 12:21-23; 18:2
- (b) Poverty and social change   Luke 1:52-53; 6:20-21, 24; Acts 2:43-47; 5:1-11
- (c) The Holy Spirit   Luke 4:18; 10:21; 11:13; Acts has been called 'Acts of the Holy Spirit', because references are so numerous throughout the book
- (d) Women   Luke 1–2; 7:37-50; 10:38-42; 23:26-31; Acts 9:36-41; 16:13-15

13 John

There can be no better illustration of the way one's presuppositions affect one's reading of Scripture than the interpretation of the Fourth Gospel. The reputation of this extraordinary work has fluctuated greatly. For many centuries its position was assured. It was believed to have been written by 'the disciple whom Jesus loved' (13:23; 21:24), one who must have had exceptionally intimate knowledge of Jesus. Therefore his gospel (it was thought) must be the most trustworthy and must take us closest to the historical reality. Then, early in the nineteenth century, came the realization that Mark (the most despised of the gospels until then) could be regarded on critical grounds as the earliest, and therefore as the most historically reliable. In which case John's gospel, which presents such a different picture from Mark's, must be regarded as a thorough reinterpretation of the facts recorded in the earliest gospel, and therefore of little historical value at all. Finally, in recent years it has been established that John's information cannot all have come from Mark or any other surviving gospel, and that after all he may preserve information at least as old and reliable as is to be found anywhere in the New Testament.

A good example of all this is the episode known as the 'cleansing of the temple'. This occurs in all four gospels: Jesus enters the temple precincts, drives out the traders, and makes certain pronouncements. In the first three gospels this incident occurs right at the end of Jesus' ministry; it is recorded as his first and only visit to Jerusalem since his public work began, and is the prelude to the culminating events of his arrest and death. But in John's gospel it stands near the beginning (2:13-22), and Jesus subsequently makes several journeys back and forth from Galilee to Jerusalem before his final appearance at the fatal Passover. These two presentations are totally irreconcilable. Can we say which is right?

Until recently there was not felt to be much of a problem. It was assumed that the earliest gospel (Mark) undoubtedly preserves the true order of events, and that John must therefore have rearranged things to suit his own purposes. But as soon as one allows for the possibility that John might in fact have had reliable information himself, doubts about Mark's order begin to make themselves felt. Is it really likely (for instance) that someone of Jesus' piety would have gone up to Jerusalem only once in two or three years, instead of regularly attending the annual festivals (as was required, at least in theory, of every devout Jew)? And are there not hints, even in Mark's gospel, that Jesus had been to Jerusalem not long before his final visit? But why then, if Mark's was not the original order of events, did Mark put the temple episode so late in the story? To which disturbing answers begin to suggest themselves. John's narrative is a complex one, weaving episodes of Jesus' popular success in Galilee into the sequence of his progressively more violent rejection by the Jerusalem authorities. In Mark things are more straightforward: success (for the most part) in Galilee followed by rejection (for the most part) in Jerusalem. But is the most straightforward narrative necessarily the most authentic? May it not be that it is Mark who has simplified rather than John who has rendered more complex? In which case it may turn out that Mark's is a gospel in which the editor had at least as much of a free hand as has been assumed to be the case in the fourth gospel.

There is another kind of evidence which again shows John to have been more of a historian, less of an inspired improviser, than used to be thought. His gospel contains a large number of place names, descriptions and references to buildings and monuments which are absent from the other gospels. The more archaeologists discover of the Jerusalem and of the Palestine of Jesus' time, the more John's 'local colour' is found to be exact. Of course this does not prove that John's narrative is *true*. It could mean only that, wishing to tell the story in his own way, he had enough knowledge of the local scene to make it sound *plausible*. But it does show that we must be prepared to take this author seriously as a historian, and not be too ready to dismiss what he tells us as intrinsically improbable.

But at this point you may want to object that we have been avoiding the main issue. Surely what makes the fourth gospel different from the others, and forces us to read it in a different way, is the manner in which it records the sayings and teaching of Jesus. To be remembered, and in due course written down, the teaching of Jesus must have been expressed in short memorable sentences – which is exactly what we find in the synoptic gospels. But in John's gospel Jesus speaks in long and elaborate paragraphs – the kind of thing which nobody could have committed to memory and which must therefore be the work of the evangelist himself, even if it was based originally on remembered sayings of Jesus. It seems to follow that whereas in the synoptic gospels we may be reading something very close to the actual words of Jesus, in John we shall always be at one remove.

Yet here again it is important not to exaggerate the contrast. There are some sayings in the fourth gospel (e.g. 'The servant is not greater than his master', 13:10) which are as terse and memorable as anything in the synoptics; and there are also complete parables in it (such as the 'Good Shepherd' in chapter 10) which are hardly to be put down to the inventive imagination of the evangelist. Moreover, the synoptic gospels themselves clearly 'edit' the sayings of Jesus on occasion. We saw how Luke deliberately strung a number of sayings together to form a section of 'table talk' – an intimate discourse over a farewell meal. The great 'farewell discourses' in John (14-17) are simply a more ambitious exercise in the same convention. Or again, it is hardly the case that the synoptic gospels have done no editing: the Sermon on the Mount in Matthew, or the discourse on the future in Mark 13, are deliberate compositions by the evangelists comparable with the discourses in John.

So the gap is not so wide as might appear at first sight. But of course we cannot possibly do away with it altogether. Even on the most casual reading the gospel of John can be seen to belong to a different world altogether from the synoptics. It is not just the form of Jesus' teaching which is new; the content also is quite different. Instead of the direct and pithy sayings directed at men's hearts and imaginations (which is the case most of the time in the synoptics) we have discourses on abstract concepts such as 'truth', 'light' and 'faith'. The readers and hearers to whom such a gospel was addressed must surely have belonged to another culture, another background altogether. Can we say anything about who these people might have been?

Oddly enough, this question is extremely difficult to answer.

It is easy enough to see that, to make sense of the gospel, they must have been familiar with concepts and ideas which would not normally have formed part of a Jewish education. Abstractions such as 'truth' or 'the Word' were common enough in places where people thought and spoke in Greek but were alien to those for whom literature consisted almost entirely of the Hebrew scriptures. The difficulty comes when we put alongside this the equally obvious fact that the gospel can hardly be appreciated without a knowledge of the Old Testament and its interpretation, and that there is hardly a page of it which does not presuppose a lively interest in, and sympathy for, Jewish institutions and ideas. We seem, in fact, to be introduced to a world that is betwixt and between – neither completely Jewish nor completely gentile. If it is Jewish, it is open to all sorts of ideas and concepts that belong to the cosmopolitan culture of the eastern half of the Roman empire; if gentile, it is clearly a society deeply influenced by the Jewish religion and way of life. Perhaps the best way to imagine it is as the kind of society which may have grown up under the influence of a flourishing synagogue. Just as, in a traditionally Christian country today, many people who would claim to have nothing to do with the church are nevertheless familiar with Christian concepts and symbols, so we can imagine that a synagogue could have had an influence which extended far beyond the official Jewish community. We know from Acts, and we can infer from Paul, that it was precisely from among these 'fringe members' of the synagogue (called 'god-fearers' in Acts) that the first Christian missionaries recruited many of their converts. Communities of this kind will have differed widely in education and culture; the one for which John's gospel was written need only have had a somewhat larger number of members with a Greek upbringing – which is precisely what one would expect in a sophisticated city like Ephesus, traditionally regarded as the home of all the New Testament writings which go under the name of John.

Can we go further and say what made the writer compose his gospel in an idiom so different from that of the synoptic gospels? Here we are on much shakier ground; but three points can be made which go some way to answering our question.

First, there is no doubt that the author deliberately paints on a much broader canvas than the other evangelists. If it is true that reading the New Testament is like overhearing the conversation of a group of people who already shared most of the important terms and ideas we find there, and whose culture and background must have been more or less the same, then the fourth gospel is one of the exceptions. Elsewhere it seems usually to have been sufficient to describe Jesus in terms borrowed from the vocabulary of the Jewish religion – the Messiah, the Son of God, the Saviour and so forth. But we must imagine that this kind of language seemed altogether too parochial and esoteric for use in a society which had received something wider than a strictly Jewish education. Jesus was surely something more significant than could be conveyed by such a limited, almost nationalistic, title as 'Messiah'. His importance was not just for the Jewish race but for all mankind, And so, to ensure that he was understood from the outset to possess this universal dimension, this writer prefaced his gospel with a description of Jesus as 'the Word', a concept that seems to have had overtones both in Jewish religion and in Greek philosophical thinking, and therefore (along with those other abstractions noticed already, such as 'truth' and 'light') to have given the reader the widest possible frame of reference for grasping the universal significance of Jesus of Nazareth.

But, *secondly*, this can only have made the task of the gospel writer more difficult. Even when Jesus was presented on a more limited scale as Messiah, it was hard enough to explain how this figure who was (in principle) so eagerly awaited by the Jewish people had in fact been rejected by all but a few; it was only by a further meditation on Scripture, and a realization of the extent to which Jesus had reinterpreted the Messiah-idea, that it was possible to acknowledge that 'it was necessary for the Messiah to suffer' (Acts 3:18). But now suppose that Jesus was not merely the saviour looked forward to by the Jewish people but a figure of universal significance; suppose there is a 'Jesus-principle' built into the very structure of the world (which is one implication of the concept of 'the Word') – how then was it possible for the world not to have acknowledged him when he appeared? The writer is fully aware of this problem: 'he came unto his own and they that were his own received him not' (1:11) is a statement in the most general terms of the challenge which confronted the writer of any gospel whatever – the fact of the rejection and execution of Jesus. Indeed this gospel keeps the issue in the foreground by representing Jesus as constantly in dispute with those who represented the official wisdom of the day in Jerusalem – a party whom he calls, for convenience, simply 'the Jews'. It is as if, again and again, Jesus is on trial; and through the arguments mounted on either side the reader can come to see both why it seemed right at the time to most people in authority to eliminate Jesus, and why, taking a longer view, we can recognize him ourselves as embodying the truth about the world.

But, *thirdly*, this 'trial' of Jesus did not end with the crucifixion and the resurrection. It still goes on every time his claims are called into question, and the defendants are his followers who 'witness' to him. It is no accident that this gospel contains a far larger section (chapters 14-17) than any of the others devoted to Jesus' instructions to his followers. In the famous 'farewell discourses' Jesus is described as preparing them for the work they will have to do when he is no longer with them, and giving them the assurance of supernatural assistance in the form of the Paraclete, the Holy Spirit. For it is in this way that John's gospel, too, speaks across the centuries to all who read it. We feel ourselves to be addressed as those who must suffer tribulation for Christ's sake and bear our witness to him in the world. In this task we shall find, as countless generations before us have found, inexhaustible resources in the gospel according to John.

PASSAGES FOR REFERENCE AND FURTHER STUDY

Cleansing of the Temple   John 2:13-22; Mark 11:15-17
'God-fearers'   Acts 13:43, 50; 17:4, 17
Local colour   John 2:20; 3:23; 4:5; 5:1-3; 9:7; 10:22-23; 18:1; 19:13, 17

14 *The Phenomenon of Jesus*

Hebrews and the 'General Epistles'

The New Testament is a book about Jesus. We expect it to tell us what sort of person he was. The first questions of a modern enquirer are usually about his life and teaching; and so we naturally tend to read the gospels first. But the earliest New Testament writers seem to have felt that there were more urgent questions to answer than straight biographical ones. They wanted to be able to explain the phenomenon of Jesus. Their most pressing task was to offer some way of understanding how this man from Nazareth could be acknowledged as the Saviour of the world.

Sometimes this concern inspired no more than a paragraph or two in a work mainly devoted to other things. The Prologue to the fourth gospel is one example. There is a rather similar essay by Paul in Colossians (1:13-20), where he attacks the notion that Christ is inferior to certain other powers in heaven and earth, and sets him majestically in the framework of the total reconciliation of the universe to its creator. The most difficult and pressing form of this question was that which concerned the death of Jesus: how could the crucifixion have been an event fraught with such fundamental consequences for mankind? There are several pages in Romans and in 1 Peter which wrestle with this question.

But there is one writing in the New Testament which takes its time to work out an answer to this question on a grand scale – the Letter to Hebrews. Not that the argument is set out under distinct headings or with a clear sense of logical progression: there was no tradition in Jewish writing for this, which is a specifically western way of conveying ideas. And there are other factors too which make it difficult for the modern reader to follow the writer's train of thought. His manner of developing arguments from Scripture is allusive and technical, and he seems constantly to turn aside from his main theme in order to deliver moral exhortations to his readers. Yet in fact this 'letter' (which is in reality more like a treatise, with only a few personal words at the end to give it even the semblance of a letter) contains a grandiose and systematic treatment of the central paradox of the Christian faith.

The author was stirred, in the first place, by a deeply religious vision. At the heart of this vision stood the temple of Jerusalem – or rather the highly significant threefold arrangement of that temple. First came a great courtyard where the people assembled for the sacrifices around the altar. In front of them was a door, screened by a curtain, through which the priests would enter the temple building itself. Inside was a chamber containing certain ritual objects – a small altar for incense, and a great seven-branched candlestick. Beyond this again stood a further curtained doorway, leading into a dark inner room – the Holy of Holies – where it was believed that God was more intensely present than anywhere else on earth. But into this room not even the priests could enter. Only the High Priest of the whole people, and he only once a year after an elaborate ritual of purification, could penetrate into that awesome sanctuary. For the rest of the year it was approached by no human being, a mysterious symbol of the brooding other-ness of God.

It was this symbol which haunted the mind of our author. He was a bookish, academic man. It was not the splendid new temple built by Herod the Great which he visualized (we cannot even be sure from his letter whether he wrote before or after the temple's destruction in AD 70) but the 'temple' of which he read in his Old Testament – no more than an arrangement of tents and curtains which was set up by Moses in the desert, and of which Herod's temple was a permanent expression in masonry. The power of the symbol lay in any case not in its architectural splendour but in the basic simplicity of its arrangement: the courtyard for the mass of the people, the ante-room for the recurring duties of the priests, and the dark mysterious sanctuary beyond, too numinous and terrible to be approached by any but a single representative of the nation on one great day of the year. The symbol worked on this writer's mind because (he was convinced) it expressed the truth about God. God *is* awesome, terrible, remote. It is impossible for human beings to draw near to the devouring fire of his presence.

Yet our author was also a Christian. In this new religion he had had an experience which he knew to be equally true, the experience of an amazing intimacy with God achieved through faith in Jesus Christ. How was this to be reconciled with that powerful and surely still valid symbol of the sheer unapproachability of God?

Could it be that the key to the mystery was after all the lonely figure of the Jewish High Priest, making his carefully prepared progress, just once a year, through the last curtain into the dark room beyond? For in itself that ritual was surely fruitless and absurd. It brought the people no nearer to the God whom they worshipped, and achieved no lasting reconciliation. But suppose its real function all along had been to lead the mind towards a new possibility? Suppose the High Priest himself, like so much in the Old Testament, was a symbol waiting to be finally 'fulfilled'? Could it be that what Jesus had done was precisely what the High Priest could never do, though he could point towards it – that he had enabled men at last to draw near to the terrible Presence by uniting them with himself who was the true High Priest?

With this question in mind our author returned to his Old Testament. Was this the meaning of the whole apparatus of priesthood and sacrifices which, though instituted by God, could no longer help men to draw near to him in faith? Was the High Priest a symbol whose meaning had now at last become intelligible through the experience of union with a Christ who was intimate with both man and God? Again and again he found (by using the techniques of interpretation which he had inherited from his Jewish education) that the pattern fitted, the correspondence worked, the Scriptures were fulfilled. And then, how much more became clear! Even the ultimate paradox of Christ's suffering could be seen to be necessary, for was not 'sacrifice' – even self-sacrifice – inherent in the very concept of priesthood?

And so, despite (as it seems to us) much stopping and starting, much turning aside with digressions and exhortations, much play upon minutiae of Old Testament texts, the great argument develops and reaches its exhilarating conclusion. Hebrews is the one consistent essay in constructive theology which we have in the New Testament, the one major attempt to explain the phenomenon of Jesus. Doubtless (as with, for example, the theological argument in Romans, which is on a comparable scale) there were particular circumstances or deviations in the Christian community which caused this author to reply with a systematic exposition; but he says so little about this that we are almost completely in the dark about the place and time of writing (as indeed people were quite soon after it was written, so much so that it was not long before, for want of a better idea, it began to be attributed to Paul). But in any case the argument stands on its own to a degree that is rare in the New Testament.

Meanwhile, alongside those who were helping the church to formulate its beliefs, there were those who were pulling in the opposite direction and attempting to make the phenomenon of Jesus fit their own pet theories and preconceived ideas. It was not long before one of the most insidious dangers pressing upon the church was found to be that of *heresy*. Up to now we have been looking at what were mainly legitimate differences of opinion within the church – it was questions of this kind which elicited most of Paul's letters. But already in Paul we can over-hear the specious suggestions of those who would have liked to make Christianity into a different sort of movement altogether. 'Do not let your minds be captured by hollow and delusive speculations' (Colossians 2:8); 'Let no one deceive you with shallow arguments' (Ephesians 5:6). It is clear that alternative explanations of the phenomenon of Jesus were being seriously canvassed, and that had these prevailed the result would have been barely recognizable as Christianity at all. It was this threat which caused the writing of most of the remaining letters in the New Testament.

Had these letters been written a century later we would know much better what the nature of the threat was. By then, the various heresies had crystallized into distinct systems of thought, and the fathers of the church had learnt how to refute them point by point. But in the New Testament period the views of the heretics are much more difficult to establish. For one thing, the letters in which we hear about them were written to church members who were already caught up in the controversy and did not need to be told what the heretics were saying. For another, the response of church leaders at this stage was not (as it was later) to meet the heretics' arguments with counter-arguments, but rather to warn their members of the consequences of abandoning the official church tradition and to point out the evident moral and spiritual inferiority of the various splinter-groups.

Consider the most impressive of all these writings: the First Letter of John. Whether the author was the same as that of the fourth gospel we do not know; all that is certain is that he knew that gospel and wrote in a similar idiom. More, he deliberately worked on some of the ideas in the gospel to show their application to the lives of Christians in the church – hence the splendid passages on love, light and truth, all concepts which have a significant place in the gospel. But behind the repeated insistence on the *moral* consequences of faith in Christ we can discern the insinuations of a party which denied that it was necessary to live in love and purity of heart in order to profess belief in Christ. For this was one of the ways in which Christianity could most easily have suffered real distortion through contact with other religious ideas of the time. There were always those who believed that religious truth must be utterly distinct from anything to do with the material circumstances of life – the body and its appetites, the emotions, or indeed any particular fact or person of history. Such people would certainly not have been able to regard Jesus – or anyone else – as the unique Saviour of the world; and we hear something of this in 1 John ('Who is the liar? Who but he who denies that Jesus is the Christ?' 2:22, compare 2 John 7). But they would also have held an utterly false view of the value of the created world. Either they would have had an almost puritanical contempt for the physical side of life and encouraged an extreme asceticism; or else they would have gone to the opposite extreme and proclaimed a kind of moral indifference which bordered on licentiousness, on the grounds that, if the body had no significance for religion, it could not matter how a person regulated (for instance) his sexual conduct. It is this second tendency which is attacked vigorously in two of the shorter letters – 2 Peter and Jude; these two writings seem in any case to be closely related to each other and to have been written in response to similar dangers threatening the church. But it was some combination of these views, allied to various kinds of speculative metaphysical systems, which almost always seems to have constituted the 'heresy' with which the churches had to contend in the New Testament period, and which elicited the warnings and exhortations contained in these so-called 'general' letters.

Which is perhaps about as much as can be said in general terms about the somewhat miscellaneous collection of writings which come in the New Testament between Hebrews and Revelation. Apart from the major ones already described (1 Peter and 1 John) there are the tiny second and third letters of John, which seem to spring from some personal difficulties between the church addressed and its leaders; and there are 2 Peter and Jude, which seem to be mainly concerned with a particular kind of heresy, and which are usually thought to have been written long after the lifetime of the apostles whose names they bear. But there is one more letter which seems to fit into no category: the Letter of James, a writing which is perhaps the most mysterious document in the whole New Testament.

We know nothing about this letter beyond what it says about itself. Traditionally, its author has been assumed to be James the brother of Jesus, who became the first leader of the church in Jerusalem. Certainly the style is distinctly Jewish; and if we try to visualize the kind of church for which such a letter would have been written, it was one which seems to have had its horizons severely limited by a somewhat parochial Jewish culture. Much of the letter is taken up with advice on how the church should conduct itself – how it should behave towards the wealthy, how it should control gossip, what it should do about the sick and the needy. Its wisdom in the main is conventional, with just a flash of illumination here and there to suggest that the teaching of Jesus had made its impact on these very traditional Jewish Christians. Just once the argument tackles a major question – that of faith and works – and tackles it from an angle so different from Paul's great treatment in Romans that one may almost imagine a debate going on between the exponents of the two opposing views – though it could equally well be taken as an attack on those who, for one reason or another, were not taking sufficiently seriously the moral implications of their new religion. There is much sound sense in the letter; but it seems a far cry from those which (like the great majority of the New Testament writings) were wrestling seriously with the one great new fact in the experience of Christians – the phenomenon of Jesus.

PASSAGES FOR REFERENCE AND FURTHER STUDY

The phenomenon of Jesus   Romans 1:1–4; 3:21–26; 5;
   Philippians 2:1-11; Colossians 1:15-23; Hebrews;
   1 Peter 1:19-21; 2:21-25

Heresy   1 Corinthians 15:12, 35; Galatians 4:8–31; Ephesians
   5:6
   Colossians 2:8; 1 Timothy 4:1-3; 2 Timothy 3:1-4:5;
   Titus 1:10-11; 2 Peter 2:1-3; 1 John 2:18-25; 2 John 7; Jude 4;
   Revelation 2:20-21

15 *The Conversation Continues*

We have been concerned in these pages with an astonishing variety of documents. They begin around the year AD 50 with Paul's earliest letters, in which we overhear some of the questioning and clarifying of issues which was going on among the first generation of Christians. They continue with Paul's major letters, in which he develops an exposition of some of the fundamental themes of the Christian faith. Next there are the gospels, which by telling the story of Jesus make up for the surprising lack of direct references to his words and works in the letters, but which at the same time inevitably and rightly introduce some interpretation of that story; and along with the gospels there is Acts, a serious essay in the history of the early church, but also (like all good history) itself an interpretation of the events it records. Then there is the polished rhetoric of the Letter to Hebrews, with its grand argument on the priestly work of Christ. There is the intimate and insistent style of the First Letter of John, applying the deep concepts of the fourth gospel to the daily life of a Christian congregation and giving earnest warnings against heresy. There are the so-called 'General Epistles': 1 Peter, with its hints of a ceremony of baptism fresh in the writer's mind, its profound meditation on the meaning of Christ's suffering and its words of encouragement to a church under some form of attack; the Letter of James, with its practical (if rather conventional) wisdom; and 2 Peter and Jude (probably written as late as the last decade of the first century), evoked by the danger of the Christian gospel being distorted by speculative thinkers outside the church. And finally there is the Book of Revelation, the one Christian essay in the *genre* called 'apocalyptic' – a splendid, poetic vision of the future, born of long meditation on similar visions in the Old Testament, and making explicit in a series of dramatic pictures some of the implications of Christian beliefs about judgement, history and forgiveness. The time span of these writings may be as much as fifty years (some scholars would say even more); geographically, they originate from all over the eastern Mediterranean from Rome in the West to Jerusalem in the East. What is it that binds them all together in such a way that we can talk about a single book: the New Testament?

This is more than an academic question. Once one realizes that these various writings were composed at different times and in different places, with perhaps as much as half a century separating the earliest from the latest, one is bound to ask the question: who collected them together into one volume, and why was it just these writings which were chosen and not any others? Why have they remained ever since uniquely authoritative for Christians?

As in so many matters connected with the New Testament, we possess very little information about its original editing and publication. No ancient author describes to us how the collection and selection took place. But we can infer that it certainly did not happen effortlessly or automatically from the fact that the position of certain writings went on being debated right into the fourth century. A few of them (Hebrews, James, Jude, for example) took many years to be fully accepted by the church, while there were two or three other writings which nearly got in but which in the end were excluded. The end-product of this gradual process was the 'canon' – that is, the New Testament as we have it today, and possessing, for Christians, an authority different in kind from that of any other writings.

On the face of it, the criterion used by the early church to decide which writings should be contained in 'scripture' and which should be excluded was very simple. Anything written by an 'apostle' was in; anything else was out. But in practice this was not quite so easy. As we have seen, the one thing we do *not* know for certain about the New Testament writings (apart from the main letters of Paul) is who wrote them – and there were already doubts about the authorship of many of them within a century of their publication. There are very few of them which were certainly written by an apostle. And those who settled the question of the canon in the early centuries were not much better placed to determine the authorship of the various books than we are.

On the other hand, the criterion begins to look more workable if we reinterpret it to mean that nothing could be admitted to the canon unless it was in some sense a *first-hand* testimony to Jesus or to the experience of the first Christians. We can still agree that on the whole the writings in the New Testament pass this test. Of course there are border-line cases. Jude and 2 Peter certainly seem to stand at one remove from the freshness of the life and faith of first-generation Christianity, and some critics would add other books to the list, such as the Pastorals. But these doubtful cases only add to one's confidence that the rest of the New Testament (the great majority of its writings and all the most important ones) do convey at first hand something unique in the history of mankind. The conversation we overhear is the conversation of those who first experienced and explored the unimaginable richness of their new faith in Christ Jesus. By comparison, the other writings which have come down to us and which *might* have been included seem to convey something distinctly second-hand.

Does this mean that the further we get ourselves from the New Testament period the harder it is to recapture the original impetus, the fainter the conversation becomes which we wish above all things to overhear?

In the normal way of things this would doubtless be so. But it is the experience of countless generations of Christians that in this case the normal rule simply does not apply. Despite all its difficulties and obscurities – despite the fact that it was written nearly two thousand years ago and belongs to a culture totally different from ours; despite its character of being, in the main, a private conversation overheard between friends rather than an appeal to mankind in general – despite all these apparent obstacles (which may seem to have been almost the main subject of this book), it still has the power to speak directly and urgently to any reader who picks it up in any place at any time. For that which ultimately caused all these various writings to be composed, preserved and collected was a new experience, a new kind of knowledge, a new way of understanding God, man and the world. The impact of this newness was such that it created (it is not too much to say) a new language, new forms of writing, new possibilities of thought, feeling and action. When we read the New Testament we expose ourselves to this newness;

indeed it becomes all the more striking and challenging as we try to enter in imagination into the circumstances in which these new things were said and done and written. This newness and freshness is a part – perhaps the major part – of what we mean by saying that Holy Scripture is 'inspired', and that its ultimate author is the Holy Spirit. It is what gives these writings – these records of conversations often only just overheard – their unique quality and power, and has ensured that the same conversations (between man and God in Christ, and between human beings themselves in the fellowship of the Holy Spirit) have continued until the present day, and will continue for as long as the New Testament has any readers at all.

A Note on Further Reading

Books on the New Testament are legion in number, but readers who wish to follow up this book are recommended to explore some of the following.

General Introductions
W. Barclay, *Introducing the Bible*, BRF & IBRA 1972
A. E. Harvey, *Companion to the New Testament: NEB*, OUP/CUP 1970
  A fuller study by the author of this book.
A. M. Hunter, *Introducing the New Testament*, SCM Press 1972
C. F. D. Moule, *The Birth of the New Testament*, A & C Black n.e. 1966
  This demands serious study, but readers will find it most rewarding.

Historical Background
R. Grant, *Historical Introduction to the New Testament*, Fontana 1971
  A full, but very readable survey.
E. Lohse, *The New Testament Environment*, SCM Press 1976
Bo Reicke, *The New Testament Era*, A & C Black 1964
  A history of New Testament times.
C. K. Barrett, *The New Testament Background*, SPCK n.e. 1974
  This is a mine of information about the background to the New Testament writings.

The Person of Jesus
C. K. Barrett, *Jesus and the Gospel Tradition*, SPCK 1967
G. Bornkamm, *Jesus of Nazareth*, Hodder & Stoughton n.e. 1973
  Not an easy book – but it provides a picture of Jesus, as seen by many modern scholars.
C. H. Dodd, *The Founder of Christianity*, Fontana 1971
  The last book written by one of the greatest of English New Testament scholars.
E. Schweizer, *Jesus*, SCM Press 1971
  A book by a leading Swiss scholar.
C. L. Mitton, *Jesus, the Fact behind the Faith*, Mowbray 1975
  An excellent introduction to the implications of modern critical study.
G. Vermes, *Jesus the Jew: a historian's reading of the Gospels*, Fontana 1976
  Interesting as giving a Jewish approach to the Gospels.

A. Richardson, *The Political Christ*, SCM Press 1973
  Takes a look at theories about Jesus' political involvement.

Interpreting the New Testament
T. G. A. Baker, *What is the New Testament?*, SCM Press 1969
  A thought-provoking book.
O. J. Lace (ed.), *Understanding the New Testament*, CUP 1965
  A useful volume for class or discussion groups.
J. A. T. Robinson, *Can we trust the New Testament?*, Mowbray 1977

Approach to New Testament Theology
T. Jeremias, *New Testament Theology:* vol. 1 *The Proclamation of Jesus*,
  SCM Press 1971
W. G. Kummel, *The Theology of the New Testament according to its major
  witnesses: Jesus – Paul – John*, SCM Press 1974
  Both Jeremias and Kummel are important – and readable.
I. H. Marshall, *The Origin of New Testament Christology*, IVP 1977
C. F. D. Moule, *The Origins of Christology*, CUP 1977

On specific subjects
A. T. Hanson, *Studies in Paul's Techniques and Theology*, SPCK 1974
C. F. D. Moule, *Worship in the New Testament*, Lutterworth 1961
C. H. Dodd, *The Apostolic Preaching and its Developments*, Hodder &
  Stoughton 1936
J. L. Houlden, *Ethics and the New Testament*, Penguin 1973
C. H. Dodd, *According to the Scriptures*, Nisbet 1952
K. Stendahl, *Paul among Jews and Gentiles*, SCM Press 1977
O. Cullmann, *The State in the New Testament*, SCM Press 1957
R. H. Lightfoot, *The Gospel Message of St Mark*, OUP Paperback 1962
J. Jeremias, *The Sermon on the Mount*, Athlone Press 1961
John Drury, *Tradition and Design in Luke's Gospel*, DLT 1976
Barnabas Lindars, *Behind the Fourth Gospel*, SPCK 1971

Index

See also references at ends of chapters 10–13